THE LADDER OF SUCCESS

A PRACTICAL GUIDE

CESAR CASTELLANOS

Originally published by Editorial Vilit & Co. Ltd.
Calle 22 C No. 31-01
Bogota, DC - Colombia, South America
Original title: La Escalera del Exito: Guia Practica

Art & Design
Fernando Gutierrez
Illustrations & Graphics
Fernando Gutierrez
Oswaldo Benavides
Julio Cesar Garcia

Copyright for this version
© 2001 by Dovewell Publications
Reprinted 2002

Translated and produced by Dovewell Communications

Dovewell Publications
Kensington Temple, Kensington Park Road
London W11 3BY England

ISBN 1-898-444-16-1

Printed in Bulgaria by POLIGRAPHIA AG-PLOVDIV

ACKNOWLEDGEMENTS

Many people have been involved in producing this manual and I want to thank all of them. Thanks to the MCI Youth Net that pioneered the vision. The Women's Net has taken great steps forward in the last three years, demonstrating that *"all things are possible to him who believes"*. The Men's Net has finally been captured by the vision, although initially finding it difficult. I want to give special thanks to Pastor Valnice Milhommens who aside from belonging to my International Twelve is our Publications Editor for Brazil. She helped us to compile the material into a practical and simple manual.

Thanks to all the pastors who have adopted the vision, believing it is from God, and desiring to see explosive growth.

Also, thanks to the Publications Department that worked on the design and the illustrations of this manual.

God has made the vision clear in all these people's lives and they have proved it by their fruit. They know that the success of the vision is not due to a method, but to the anointing of God.

Cesar Castellanos

the ladder of success
a practical guide

CONTENTS

the ladder of success
a practical guide

INTRODUCTION

"Then the Lord answered me and said: 'Write the vision and make it plain on tablets, that he may run who reads it. For the vision is yet for an appointed time; but at the end it will speak, and it will not lie. Though it tarries, wait for it; because it will surely come, it will not tarry'".
(Habakkuk 2:2-3)

The prophet Habakkuk experienced tremendous warfare in prayer. He complained to God saying: *"Why do You make men like fish of the sea, like creeping things that have no ruler over them?"* *(Habakkuk 1:14)*
God answered his question by revealing to him that there would be a governmental vision where the believers would not be like fish in the sea or like fierce reptiles, without anyone to rule over them.
I believe that the best model to see this leadership prophecy fulfilled, and church growth, is the GOVERNMENT OF TWELVE. This is why we have prepared this manual for you. It will help your ministry to experience growth that is beyond your imagination.
It is your responsibility to ensure that your team makes a supreme effort to pursue the vision without delay, for this is a time of grace.

Cesar Castellanos

the ladder of success a practical guide

PREFACE

I remember being a student in a Bible Institute. We were a group of young people wanting to serve the Lord, but also fooling about and playing jokes on each other. Once we were divided into groups to study and expound certain Bible texts. Our group was given the passage of the raising of Lazarus.

We studied the passage in detail and believed we had discovered something new. We now knew how to raise the dead! We wondered what we were going to call this great revelation when we explained it to the whole class. We decided to call it *"Four Steps To Raising the Dead"*. In reality it was a very simple formula. We said: "If it worked for Jesus, it should work for us."

Many in our class were upset at the title. Someone said, *"It sounds like a food recipe!"* We found the whole exercise very creative and amusing. Many years have passed since then and much has changed in us. We now know that Jesus did not perform miracles simply by following a method. We know that the Holy Spirit was with Him. *"How God anointed Jesus of Nazareth with the Holy Spirit and power, who went about doing good and healing all who were oppressed by the Devil, for God was with Him" (Acts 10:38).* God listened to Jesus because of His reverent fear: *"[Jesus], in the days of His flesh, offered up prayers and supplications, with vehement cries and tears to Him who was able to save Him from death, and was heard because of His godly fear" (Hebrews 5:7).* Jesus did not follow His own will but the Father's: *"Jesus said to them, 'My food is to do the will of Him who sent Me, and to finish His work'" (John 4:34).*

For a long time we have not wanted to write manuals about our work. Our priority is for people to capture the spirit of the work, understand the role of character in the vision and the importance of the anointing of God for its success.

Many leaders constantly look for a method to bring about growth and blessing. They want someone to tell them two or three principles and then, as if by magic, a successful ministry would appear. In reality, success is the product of daily discipline that produces the character of Christ.

When I first taught on the Ladder of Success, it was not my intention to provide a formula, nor do we intend to do so in this book. Our intention is to form in each believer a lifestyle that will leave the fragrance of Christ everywhere and to make soul winners and disciple makers according to the commandment of our Lord Jesus Christ.

Manuals deal with methods and structures - instructions on how to do things. But the Christian life deals mainly with attitudes and heart's intentions. God sees the attitude of our hearts. For this reason I want to mention some things that you need in order to read this book effectively and for your ministry to be successful.

First of all, capture the spirit of the vision. Let it reach the depths of your being. Pray as you are reading and let the Holy Spirit speak to your heart.

Secondly, seek a deep understanding. I hope that when you have read this book each page will be full of your notes, questions and underlining.

Thirdly, begin to apply whatever the Holy Spirit shows you in your personal life and ministry.

Finally, share it with your disciples. You always learn something new when you are preparing to teach others. If you learn something and it changes you, you have made progress, but if you learn something and it changes others, you are changing the world.

It is our prayer that when you finish reading this book, you will not say, *"Now I know what they do in Colombia",* but that a prophetic fire will be kindled in your heart. *"Then I said, 'I will not make mention of Him, nor speak any more in His name.' But His word was in my heart like a burning fire shut up in my bones; I was weary of holding it back, and I could not"* *(Jeremiah 20:9).*

Cesar Fajardo

PREFACE TO THE UK EDITION

There is no doubt in my mind that the Church in the 21st Century is going through tremendous changes. In fact, these changes are nothing short of revolutionary, and, surely, there is no other option but to change. We have to return to the principles of the Church of the 1st Century. We must see the vibrancy of the early church restored to the Church of today.

The challenge of world evangelism is intensifying. Nowhere is this more apparent than in Britain and Europe at this time. We are living in a post-modern culture, influenced by a post-Christian and secular mindset, surrounded by ethnic unrest and increasingly dominated by anti-Christian laws and hardening governmental attitudes.

But into this field of conflict, God is bringing His revolution. It's a revolution of love, power and the first principles of Christ. He is raising up a church that is true to the Great Commission - to make, mature and mobilise disciples. It's a church that is prepared to abandon the trammelled traditions of the past and forge itself into new models of meeting and ministering together and, above all, new methods of re-evangelising and re-capturing the hearts of more than 600 million people in Europe who are without Christ.

The model of the Government of 12, pioneered in the International Charismatic Mission, Bogota by Pastor Cesar Castellanos, is a vision for our times. Many church leaders in Europe are now beginning to understand that the cell church model is not just for Latin America, but it is firmly grounded in the New Testament. Cell churches are among the largest and fastest growing Christian communities in the world - whether in South America, South Korea, North America, Asia, Africa or Europe.

The work of the Holy Spirit through Pastor Cesar is set to shake not only Colombia, but also the nations of the world. The Government of 12 is not a humanly-engineered strategy. It is a vision based on a divinely ordered principle. It represents for us today the restoration of true apostolic and governmental authority and spiritual effectiveness to the body of Christ on earth. We are proving this in Kensington Temple, London City Church. Since we adopted the model of 12 and implemented this vision, our church has been transformed and we are on the way to fulfilling our mission: London and the world for Christ.

I am profoundly grateful to Pastor Cesar, not just for the G12 Vision, but also for his gracious and godly influences upon my life personally. This book, 'The Ladder of Success', takes us to the heart of the G12. The principles it presents are sound, biblical and proven. The teaching is simple and practical, making it easy to apply it to your life and implement it in your church.

It is a great joy to present to you this UK edition. It is my prayer that God will use 'The Ladder of Success' to transform your life, your church and your community for Christ. And, more than that, I pray it will fuel the fires of revival across the continent of Europe and the nations of the world.

Colin Dye
London, October 2001

THE POWER
OF A VISION

Chapter 1

THE POWER OF A VISION

BASIC BIBLE FOUNDATION

"I will make you into a great nation; I will bless you and make your name great; and you will be a blessing" (Genesis 12:2).

As soon as you start to walk the Christian path as a disciple of Jesus Christ and a practitioner of His teaching, a veil is lifted from your mind and your heart. God makes you into a visionary and your view of life changes.

When God created the world and mankind, He did so by using His incomparable and unique creative power. First He had a vision of what He wished to do in creation. This vision served as a plan of action to achieve the purposes of His heart: *"For we are His workmanship" (Ephesians 2:10).* The Lord stamped His character on us and made us partakers of His own nature. He made us after His own image and likeness and gave us a creative capacity. This will only become effective for our lives and our work in the church if we dare to become visionaries. Vision is the determining factor in success. In the Bible we see that God always chooses a man to accomplish His purposes. He reveals His will to a man, gives him His plan and surrounds him with people of the same heart. These people support him in the work, becoming the strength behind the vision. God loves to partner with a man or a woman who dares to believe and is willing to obey Him.

the ladder of success
a practical guide

WHAT IS DIVINE VISION?

It is God's idea revealed to the mind of man as a goal to be achieved.

Everything that exists has its origin in God's vision of creation. In giving a vision to man the Lord expects him to fight to see it fulfilled. Vision is the divine plan of action that drives leaders to overcome every difficulty and shape a nation's destiny. The concept of vision has been known since the beginning of creation. It was God's own idea that brought everything into being, including His greatest vision: man himself.
"Then God said 'Let Us make man in Our image, according to Our likeness'" (Genesis 1:26).
Vision also consists of having a clear image of who God wants me to be and what He wants me to do. It is through faith that I enter the spiritual realm and receive that vision from God. I bring it down to the natural realm through faith and with the Holy Spirit's help.

GOD WORKS THROUGH YOU

God lives in you and wants you to keep His Word. When you start to doubt, God's power is weakened in you, and the Holy Spirit is grieved. When you believe God's Word, despite the circumstances, the power of God is free to work.
"...the desire of the righteous will be granted".
(Proverbs 10:24)

HAVE A CLEAR VISION OF WHAT YOU WANT

When you pray, form a mental picture as clear as the one on your television screen. When you see a blurred picture on your television screen, you know that something is wrong with either the signal or the TV set. In the same way, if you do not have a clear vision, something is wrong with the signal (your faith) or in your life, whether it's fear, doubt or sin.

RAISE YOUR FAITH LEVEL

Faith is not intellectual; it is spiritual. It goes beyond our understanding and everything around us. It has to spring up from your innermost being, where your heart's desire is joined to God's will as revealed in His Word and from prayer, until you reach the assurance that God has heard you. *"Delight yourself also in the Lord, and He shall give you the desires of your heart" (Psalm 37:4).*

EXPECT A MIRACLE

When we know that our need is in God's hand, the only thing we have to do is wait. Miracles are the result of a battle in the spiritual realm won through faith. When God said to me *"Dream of a big church"*, I was able to realise that the size of the church was not outside, but inside me, and whatever I was able to believe Him for, God would give me. After Abraham received God's promise of a son, he had to feed this promise by faith. He had to strengthen himself daily in God, continually battling with a spirit of unbelief. Like a stubborn intruder unbelief continuously attacked the patriarch's mind, but he never gave in to it. His unbelief would have aborted the birth of his future generations.

"As it is written, 'I have made you a father of many nations' in the presence of Him whom he believed - God, who gives life to the dead and calls those things which do not exist as though they did; who, contrary to hope, in hope believed, so that he became the father of many nations, according to what was spoken, 'So shall your descendants be'". (Romans 4:17-18) Abraham did not weaken in faith. "He did not waver at the promise of God through unbelief, but was strengthened in faith, giving glory to God, and being fully convinced that what He had promised He was also able to perform" (Romans 4: 20-21).

CHARACTERISTICS OF GOD'S VISION

You can recognise a vision that comes from God because it has certain characteristics: its motivation is pure and not self-seeking. It contributes towards the social and spiritual well-being of the community. A true vision does not promote self, but praises God and brings glory to Jesus Christ. God wants us to take hold of the vision to fulfil His purpose on earth.

The following characteristics of a God-given vision will help us take part in the fulfilment of His purposes:

VISION IS THE MOTIVATION BEHIND GREAT LEADERS

God's vision makes us victors. The successful leader wants to know the Lord's purpose for his life and does all he can to carry it out. This victory is won when he starts to guard his thoughts and makes every effort to have the mind of Christ.

See Philippians 4:8.

VISION IS THE POWER FOR REVIVAL

To enter the divine vision means to remain in the spiritual realm, so that we can see from that position what we desire to happen in the natural realm. This is the only way we can see things from God's point of view and call that which is not as if it was.

Just as Ezekiel realised in the vision of the valley of dry bones we need to understand that the only way we are going to make a change in our lives and our ministries is through divine intervention.
See Ezekiel 37:1-9.

A SUCCESSFUL LEADER CAN REPRODUCE THE VISION IN OTHERS

The Lord Jesus' vision was to redeem humanity from condemnation. Apart from Him, there is no other hope for mankind. Jesus had a vision of saving us by paying a very high price: shedding His blood and dying on the cross of Calvary.

Our work is to take this vision of Jesus and reproduce it in others, sharing the message of salvation.
"Deliver those who are drawn toward death, and hold back those stumbling to the slaughter"
(Proverbs 24:11).

the ladder of success
a practical guide

IDENTIFY WITH THE VISION

You now understand what a vision is and the qualities that identify it as God's vision. It is important that you also know that the vision of God is related to leadership and ministry. If you have a pure heart and correct attitude, God will bless you and prosper the work of your hands. The burning desire of your heart should be to win your city and your nation for Christ through the Government of 12 by making every believer a leader able to reproduce the work of God.

We need to understand that the vision is:

To win souls and make disciples

You must desire to produce rapid church growth in your city and nation. Reaching people for the gospel is not enough, they must be formed into disciples of Jesus and through the G12 model produce fruit that lasts.

The goal is:

To make every believer a leader

We have been implementing the vision for some years, not allowing "opting out". Everyone is encouraged to attain a leadership qualification in a short time through the School of Leaders. This entire process is developed through steps that we call *The Ladder of Success,* which consists of: *win, consolidate, disciple and send.* The model is based on the biblical principle of *"the Twelve".*

HOW THE VISION CAME

During the first seven years of ministry we tried to develop the cell vision on the model of Dr. Cho's church in Korea. However, the cell growth was slow. After seven years we had only around 70 cells, with only 30% of the church members involved. We did not know about homogeneous groups, and we did not bear the fruit we wanted.
I turned to the Lord in prayer, because I knew that there had to be another way to implement the vision. It was then that the Lord gave me a specific word. He said: "I will give you the capacity to rapidly train your people". This eventually led to the establishment of the School of Leaders. Later on He lifted the veil from my mind and revealed the reason for the groups of twelve.
How many people did Jesus disciple?
This was the first question that came to my mind.
I thought about the passages that spoke about Jesus' contact with the multitudes. One day He would be with a particular group, the next day with another. But the only group with whom the Lord always remained was the twelve whom He had called.
Why twelve? Why not eleven or thirteen? Why did He not concentrate on equipping multitudes? Why did He spend all His energy in enabling twelve? What secret is there in twelve?
While asking these questions, the Lord lifted the veil further and revealed to me what we are working with today, and which is now being implemented in other nations: the Government of Twelve.
God's words came very clearly into my life, saying: *"Train twelve people and reproduce in them the character of Christ which is in you. And if every one of them does the same with another twelve people, and if these, in their turn, do the same with another twelve, transmitting the same vision to each other, you and your church will experience unprecedented growth" (Fig 1).*

I began to see in my mind the success that we would have in our ministry in a short time. Later on God showed me the explosive growth that He wanted to give us in a vision, and that in one year we would experience exceptional growth. When I saw this vision all I could say was *"My God, this is something extraordinary!"*

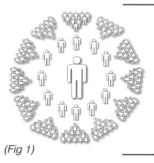

(Fig 1)

The Pastor...

- *Imparts character to*
- *Leads*
- *Prepares*
- *Motivates*
- *Corrects*
- *Sends*

...*his twelve*

The model of the Twelve has always been in the heart of God. The number twelve is symbolic of government. In the Bible, each number has its own significance. The number three symbolises the Trinity, the number four symbolises what is worldly, the number seven symbolises perfection etc. In the same way, the number twelve symbolises government that comes from God.

In the beginning God established twelve months to govern the year. The days are governed by two periods of twelve hours. God also established twelve tribes to rule over the nation of Israel.

The G12 model has been implemented:

IN ADMINISTRATION

King Solomon had twelve governors, and each one was obliged to supply him and his household with provisions for a month every year.

See 1 Kings 4:7.

IN RESTORATION

In the time of Elijah, Israel was practising idolatry and was apostate. The prophet Elijah zealously challenged the prophets of Baal. He challenged them to demonstrate the power of their idols before the nation and to let the true God respond by fire. Elijah began to rebuild the altar of Jehovah, which was in ruins.

"And Elijah took twelve stones, according to the number of the tribes of Jacob ...Then with the stones he built an altar in the name of the Lord..."
(1 Kings 18: 31a & 32a).

After rebuilding the altar, he offered a sacrifice to God. God did not delay in answering the prophet. He answered by fire and through this act the nation was reconciled to God.

The model of the Twelve restores the altar of God that is in ruins. The altar of God is destroyed in most nations. We need men and women, zealous for God, who will dedicate themselves to work, not on the walls or structures of some building, but for the people for whom Christ shed His blood. The altar of God within their hearts is in ruins because of the bad example of some religious leaders. Many people have walked away from God, because they have become disappointed in their faith.

IN RECONCILIATION

It is not a coincidence that the last pages of the last book in the Old Testament express the purpose of Elijah's ministry, saying:

"Behold, I will send you Elijah the prophet before the coming of the great and dreadful day of the Lord. And he will turn the hearts of the fathers to the children, and the hearts of the children to their fathers, lest I come and strike the earth with a curse" (Malachi 4:5-6).

the ladder of success
a practical guide

I am convinced that in these final days God will release an Elijah anointing that will fall like a mantle over all the earth.

This anointing will move Christian leaders from different parts of the world to act with the same spirit as Elijah, with reconciliation within the family as a priority. God wants leaders to be instruments in His hands to bring peace into millions of homes that are on the verge of collapse.

IN THE STRUCTURE OF THE NATION OF ISRAEL

God revealed Himself to Moses as the God of Abraham, Isaac and Jacob. Abraham is the man of faith, Isaac the man of sacrifice and Jacob the man of government. Notice that the promise of God to Abraham did not come to pass until the government of the twelve was established. The Bible says, *"from Isaac your descendants will come."* But Isaac had to have Jacob and Jacob had to have twelve sons, who became the twelve patriarchs. Each one of Jacob's sons became a tribe and the twelve tribes of the nation of Israel came into being. When the twelve tribes were united the nation of Israel was strengthened and prospered, but when disunity came, the nation was weakened, oppressed and overpowered by their enemies and dispersed throughout the earth.

THE LORD'S EXAMPLE

Jesus invested most of His ministry on earth in shaping the character and ministry of twelve disciples. Jesus did not teach and disciple the multitudes. His contact with the multitudes was sporadic. When He was among the people He met their needs. He healed multitudes, delivered them, ministered to them, taught them, but He did not form them. It is easier to disciple twelve people than all the people who heard the Sermon on the Mount.

Jesus concentrated on shaping twelve men, in order to reproduce His character in them. For this to happen many religious ideas had to be demolished. This is why Jesus moved away from the conventional. He did not look for His twelve in the best theological colleges. Jesus chose His twelve after a night of prayer. Likewise we cannot choose our twelve because they are our friends. We cannot choose them for their intellect, nor for the way they pray, nor for human abilities or talents. We must choose our twelve because the Holy Spirit confirms that they are faithful and that they are the right ones. Jesus took them in His hands and started moulding them, as the potter moulds the clay. For three and a half years He worked on the disciples' character. Through His teaching He cleansed them from all impurities. At the same time He sowed eternal truths into them, so that when He was no longer with them, they were able to depend totally on the Holy Spirit, just as Jesus had done.

The twelve that followed the Lord became the strong pillars on which the Christian faith would rest. The Lord worked through these twelve because He knew it is the most efficient form of pastoring people. The Lord won these twelve in prayer. He consolidated them, He discipled them and then He sent them.

IT IS ABOUT RELATIONSHIP

In the model of the Twelve it is imperative that we hold weekly meetings. Our priority is to build relationships. People do not come to talk about business matters, but the emphasis is on being sensitive to the guidance of the Holy Spirit, the spiritual needs of the team and the development of their ministry.

the ladder of success

a practical guide

Jesus had a strong relationship with His twelve. He could detect anything that was out of order, and in this type of relationship continual ministry is needed. Your relationship with the twelve allows you to get to know them in a very personal way. They have to go through a process of inner healing and deliverance, for it is absolutely vital to break chains and the power of curses. If someone has never been ministered to, he cannot minister to others.

CHOOSE THOSE WHO BEAR FRUIT

You should not choose your twelve because of friendship or because you have known them for a long time, but because of their fruit. First of all we form cells. The most outstanding leaders who reproduce twelve cells in one year and who faithfully follow the model are the ones qualified to be in our twelve. They have earned their leadership. From the beginning we need to ensure that our twelve are people who have captured the vision, bear fruit and multiply.

EVERYONE IS A SOUL WINNER

The twelve need to know how to evangelise. They need to know how to seek souls. Where are the lost? How do we minister to them? They need to have evangelistic strategies to reach these people.

THEY SHOULD DEVELOP THEIR WORK IN A HOMOGENEOUS MANNER

This is what we began to implement. A young person should win another young person, a man should win another man, a woman another woman, a couple another couple and the children other children.
For a while we worked with non-homogeneous cells in different areas of Bogota. We realised that the growth was too slow and that homogeneous groups resulted in greater multiplication.

THE PASTORAL WORK IS STRENGTHENED

Your twelve become like your assistant pastors.
There is unity. The leaders of the twelve have no
interest in usurping the pastor's position. Instead,
everyone works together as a team to promote the
vision. An interesting thing is that through the vision
the Lord has made us a family with great affection
and respect for one another. We find that one
group will support another group. The stronger
will support the weaker. Above all there is always
mutual respect.

THE LADDER OF SUCCESS

win
consolidate
disciple
send

"The Ladder of Success is the process whereby success is guaranteed to everyone prepared to consecrate themselves to working with cells.

Just as plants need four fundamental elements (Nitrogen, Potassium, Lime and Phosphoric Acid) in order to develop and produce fruit, so in the in the Christian life, there are four steps which, when carefully applied, bring real results."

Cesar Castellanos

win

WIN

"The fruit of the righteous is a tree of life, and he who wins souls is wise" (Proverbs 11:30).

God's burning desire is for souls. For this reason evangelism should become an art, where God's timing, the anointing and sensitivity to the Holy Spirit are combined to reach the lost. Since souls are eternal we need to ask God to make us experts in the art of winning souls.

- *Winning* is a process through which we proclaim the gospel to every person in a way that leads to true repentance.
- *It is a privilege* that God has entrusted us with as those who have been redeemed by the blood of the Lamb. The prophet Daniel said, *"Those who are wise shall shine like the brightness of the firmament, and those who turn many to righteousness like the stars forever and ever" (Daniel 12:3).*
- *It is an act of humility.* Jesus had to leave His throne of glory. He became man, and thus granted us eternal redemption.
  See Philippians 2:5-8.
- *It is a demonstration of love:* *"...he who turns a sinner from the error of his way will save a soul from death and cover a multitude of sins" (James 5:20).*
- *It is a need:* *"For if I preach the gospel, I have nothing to boast of, for necessity is laid upon me; yes, woe is me if I do not preach the gospel! For if I do this willingly, I have a reward; but if against my will, I have been entrusted with a stewardship" (1 Corinthians 9:16-17).*

A whole army is needed to share the gospel. It should be made up of men and women who have been saved and transformed by the redeeming blood of the Lamb and whose passion is to win souls.

Charles Spurgeon said, *"If I was totally selfish and was only concerned with my own happiness, even so, I would be concerned to win souls for Christ. Because I have never known such an indescribable joy, pure and overflowing which filled my heart, the day that someone came to know his Saviour through me."*

R A Torrey testified, *"I knew very little of the joy of salvation until someone accepted Christ for the first time through me."*

Paul said, *"To the weak I become as weak, that I might win the weak. I have become all things to all men, that I might by all means save some"* *(1 Corinthians 9:22).*

The apostle did not limit the gospel. He determined to become a great strategist in order to reach people, no matter what their social position, culture or ethnic origin.

"He who wins souls is wise" *(Proverbs 11:30).* What is wisdom? To win souls. It does not say *"He who makes money is wise"*, nor *"he who studies in the best universities is wise"*. No - only he who wins souls is wise. Many souls are lost because the person who has been sent does not know how to present the gospel of Jesus Christ.

"...who desires all men to be saved and to come to the knowledge of the truth" *(1 Timothy 2:4).*

REASONS WHY WE SHOULD WIN OTHERS FOR JESUS

BECAUSE OF THEIR WORTH TO GOD

"For what will it profit a man if he gains the whole world, and loses his own soul?" (Mark 8:36).
A soul is worth much more than the whole world, than all the stars put together. The value of a soul cannot be measured. God can destroy the stars and create them again, but He cannot do that with the soul. God cannot destroy a soul and replace it with another.
"The soul who sins shall die" (Ezekiel 18:4).
"For all have sinned and fall short of the glory of God" (Romans 3:23).

JESUS PAID A HIGH PRICE

"Knowing that you were not redeemed with corruptible things, like silver or gold, from your aimless conduct received by tradition from your fathers, but with the precious blood of Christ, as of a Lamb without blemish and without spot"
(1 Peter 1:18-19).

FAITH IN JESUS CHRIST IS THE ONLY WAY TO SALVATION

"Therefore, I said to you that you would die in your sins; for if you do not believe that I am He, you will die in your sins" (John 8:24).
"Then Jesus said to them, 'When you lift up the Son of Man, then you will know that I am He, and that I do nothing of Myself; but as My Father has taught Me, I speak these things. And He who sent Me is with Me. The Father has not left me alone, for I always do those things that please him'" (John 8: 28-29).

UNDERSTANDING OUR CALLING

"I am a debtor both to Greeks and to barbarians, both to wise and to unwise" (Romans 1:14). Paul said that he must preach the gospel of Jesus Christ to everyone. Without shame, he gave himself completely to the preaching of the gospel - not caring about who would reject him. It is said that the great evangelist John Knox used to constantly intercede for the salvation of the lost in his nation. His cry was *"God, give me Scotland or I die."* When we understand the seriousness of our calling we will not rest until we fulfil the purpose of God in our land. In order to become a winner of souls, you must:

BE REDEEMED

You need to reach the point where you feel that you are the greatest sinner on earth and know that only the blood of Jesus can save you. You have to acknowledge your sins, confess them, renounce them and ask for God's restoring grace in your life.

HAVE COMPASSION FOR THE LOST

We should feel the same way that Jesus did.

EQUIP YOURSELF WITH THE WORD

Each one of us has a responsibility to share with others what God has done in our lives. In order to do this we should prepare ourselves and know how to use the word of truth. We should train as soldiers so that we know how to use our weapons correctly. The word of truth is a two-edged sword, but it can be useless if not handled properly.

BE FILLED WITH THE HOLY SPIRIT

This is very different from just believing in Him, because the fullness of the Spirit is the fruit of being completely yielded to Him. Jesus was able to change the course of history in just three and a half years because He lived in the fullness of the Holy Spirit. It is better to live one day in the fullness of the Spirit than one thousand in your own strength.

BE A GOOD TESTIMONY

There are many people who say one thing but do the opposite. Your life must be an open book where people can read your actions without caring too much about your words.

BECOME IMMERSED IN THE VISION

Many Christians have a passive attitude, believing that their financial support for the kingdom of God is enough. But God's cry is *"Whom shall I send, and who will go for Us?"* Our response should be *"Here am I! Send me" (Isaiah 6:8)*. To be filled with the vision makes us reproducers of life, which is God's will for all the members of the church.

TESTIFY TO OTHERS ABOUT CHRIST

This is to give life to the vision and to go out to reach all those that the Lord will put in your path.

the ladder of success
a practical guide

WINNING IN THE CELL

Definition of a cell:

Small groups made up of people who meet together at least once a week, focusing on the Word of God and with the purpose of development and growth.

In these groups we find: a host (who provides the place), a leader (the person who is capable of directing the cell), an assistant (the leader's right-hand person), the participants (all the active members and those people invited to the meeting). The cells are small centres that teach the Scriptures in a simple and practical manner, and where people who attend are built up. This includes those non-believers who, week after week, are won for Christ. This cell principle has worked since the early church when the growth of the congregation came through the cells.

"Then the word of God spread, and the number of the disciples multiplied greatly in Jerusalem" (Acts 6:7).

"...I kept back nothing that was helpful, but proclaimed it to you, and taught you publicly and from house to house, testifying to Jews, and also to Greeks, repentance toward God and faith toward our Lord Jesus Christ" (Acts 20:20-21).

IMPORTANCE OF THE CELL VISION

Above all, remember that opening the door of your house to host a cell is like taking the Ark or presence of God into your home. You are striving to reach a whole community with the light of the gospel. If you are faithful in the little things (a cell) the Lord will surely place you in charge of big things.

THE SUCCESS OF THE CHURCH IS IN THE CELLS

The success of a church which adopts the cell vision can be seen in numerical and spiritual growth. This growth comes because the cell vision helps to form and equip disciples who will take upon themselves the task of spreading the gospel to the world.

THE CELLS FACILITATE ONE-TO-ONE PASTORING

Jesus was always concerned with meeting the needs of each person. He developed His ministry through contact with people and was not limited by buildings, as we see in Mark 6:34. The cell vision allows us to act as Jesus did. Even the newest believer can meet with his family and a cell leader can pastor each person individually.

PASTORAL WORK BECOMES EASIER

The work does not fall onto just one person's shoulders. When a pastor manages to involve the whole church in cells, the results are better. Each member of the congregation will always feel looked after.

THE CELLS ARE THE BACKBONE OF THE CHURCH

Within the cell life there must be evangelistic activity. Every department in the church must operate through the cells. It is there where souls are reached and the ministry is done. At the same time in the cell members are prepared to be useful in cell multiplication and ministry *(See 1 Peter 5:10)*.

IT IS THE MINE WHERE LEADERS OF TWELVE COME FROM

The cells are the best place to form leaders from whom we can select our teams of twelve. We can choose from the people that meet weekly with us in a house, an office or a workshop. We choose those who are most successful in producing fruit and consider them to join our basic group of twelve who support us in ministry *(See Luke 6:12-17)*.

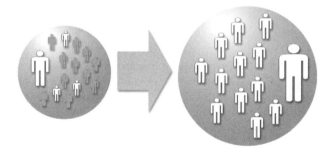

You discover who are the best leaders in the cell – those who produce most fruit – and choose them to form your G12.

Jesus won twelve men in whom He reproduced His character and who became His representatives to the whole world. He transmitted His vision to the twelve so that they could in turn transmit it to twelve others. In this way He achieved multiplication.

MULTIPLICATION

The new cell begins to form with some of the members of the original cell. Six people is a good number to start a cell.

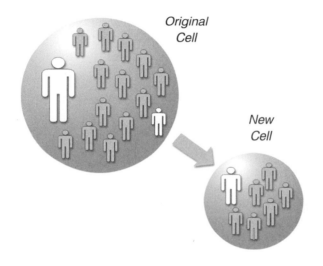

Original Cell

New Cell

Multiplication: Product of two factors.

Multiplying :   Leader (agent of change)
Multiplier: Holy Spirit (supernatural action)

Multiplication should be presented as in
Matthew 14:13-21:
Five loaves and two fishes to feed 5000.
The proportion is 1:1000, counting only men, a task
which can only be achieved by the Holy Spirit.

the ladder of success
a practical guide

THE PURPOSE OF CELLS

A.   To open the doors for people to be saved.
        See Acts 10.
B.   To allow people to identify with the
        leadership. *See Matthew 9:10.*
C.   To offer the opportunity to receive a touch
        from God. *See Luke 5:19-20.*

THE IDEAL CELL

For an ideal cell we should:

*Prepare a message specific to the
needs of the homogeneous group,
men, women, young people,
or children.*

*Have a host and leader committed
to the vision.*

Have financial goals.

Have twelve people.

This will help us to achieve our goals. Each person
will be able to take responsibility and together we
can work as a team and develop strategies.

WINNING THROUGH THE CELL

Since the cell is the main arm of the church to penetrate the community with the gospel of Jesus Christ, the majority of decisions for Christ will come through the cells. Some strategies can be applied to accelerate the harvest of souls.

THE ONE-MONTH PRAYER TRIPLET

Why, in *Daniel 6:7,* did Satan give a plan to Daniel's enemies to stop him praying for a month? If the prophet stopped praying he would certainly fail. Lack of prayer brings death, but Daniel's persevering thirty-day prayer released life. When we commit ourselves to pray continuously for a whole month for unbelievers the Spirit of God will respond with mercy and give them life.

■ *The leader who is planning to form a cell takes two others (they can be believers).*

■ *Each one of them, in prayer, targets three more people.*

■ *All the members of the group also get three names from the other members. These could be friends, work mates, neighbours, or family members.*

■ *They meet for an hour a week for four weeks and in their meeting they pray specifically for the conversion of those people. They pray also for the existing group members as well as for those who will join them. It is important to have a time of fasting and intercession and to engage in spiritual warfare to see people saved. They bind every power that is in opposition to salvation and neutralise them in the name of Jesus. They ask for every spirit that blocks*

the ladder of success
a practical guide

the revelation of the gospel to be bound and destroyed in the name of Jesus, and that the Lord will convict people of sin and bring them to repentance. Every member of the group should therefore be praying for the salvation of nine people at one time.

CONTACT THROUGH FRIENDSHIP EVANGELISM

After thirty days of prayer, each person is contacted and special interest is shown in them. God's love for them is shared. Then it is good to introduce the plan of salvation, with the help of four spiritual laws:

1) God loves you and has a wonderful plan for your life.

2) Man is a sinner and therefore separated from God.

3) Jesus Christ is the only bridge between God and man.

4) We should personally accept Jesus Christ as our Lord and Saviour.

LEADING THEM TO JESUS

After sharing the four spiritual laws, we can lead the person to pray a prayer of commitment. This is when the person surrenders his life completely to Jesus. The following prayer may act as guideline:
"Father, today I acknowledge that I am a sinner. I repent for every sin that I have commited. I renounce and turn from my sinful life. I ask that the blood of Jesus Christ would wash away all my sins and cleanse me from my rebellion. Lord Jesus, today, I open my heart. I invite you to come into my life and ask that from now on you will be my Lord and Saviour. Thank you for saving me and giving me eternal life. Amen".

After prayer:

■ *Offer the booklet "Encounter".*
Ask them to carefully read it.
■ Show them how to read the *First Letter of John* at the end of the booklet. Comment on the importance of reading the letter every day, during a whole week, in order to understand it.

CELL MEETINGS

Invite your friend along to a cell meeting. It is with these friends that the cell begins to take shape. Until now, the cell has been in embryonic form – three believers meeting to pray for the conversion of their friends. Once their friends begin to attend the cell enters into the formation stage. The cell meeting adopts the normal programme including the preaching of the Word of God.

CELEBRATIONS IN THE CHURCH

Mention the different meetings held in the church and invite them to come. Explain the importance of meeting together regularly and attending the different events. We should always do this with a spirit of encouragement and not putting any pressure on them, as that can be counter-productive.

SPECIAL EVENTS

Invite the person who has been won in the cell to participate in special evangelistic events. The cell will always continue to seek the lost with the aim of bringing them to Christ. What happened with the first three people should be reproduced in every new member.

This way new believers should be introduced into the cell every week.

One strategy is to keep a vacant chair in the meeting reserved for a new person who could be there, but isn't. Everyone should pray for that person to attend the next meeting. The cell should aim to win at least one new believer every week.

WINNING THROUGH THE CHURCH MEETINGS

THE ALTAR CALL

These are two very important things:

- *An altar call for salvation should be made at every meeting.*
- *The message of the cross should be presented when making the altar call.*

After the preaching everyone should join the speaker in the prayer of commitment. The following prayer of salvation can help:

"Lord Jesus, I look towards the cross of Calvary where you gave your life for me. I acknowledge that you are the Son of the living God. You took upon yourself my sin, my guilt, my condemnation, my curse, my sicknesses and my death. It should have been me dying on that cross. Lord Jesus, I renounce sin, the world and the Devil. I repent of my sins and I ask your forgiveness for having offended you. I renounce all past links with the powers of darkness, and I open my life to you. I confess with my mouth that you are the Son of God, who died my death, but rose again triumphant and victorious. Jesus, today I open my heart and I accept you as my Lord and my Saviour. Reign in my life from this day forward. Amen."

After the prayer:

- *Invite those that prayed this prayer for the first time to go into a separate room.*
- *The preacher should briefly speak about the love of God, the consequences of sin, Christ as the only and sufficient Lord and Saviour, the blessings of repentance and the benefits of accepting Christ.*

For example:

"There are some things which you need to know:

- *God loves you and proved His love by sending His only Son to die for you.*
- *The Bible says that all have sinned and are separated from God and that includes you.*
- *Jesus came into this world as the Son of Man so that you could become a son of God.*
- *Jesus became sin on the cross so that you could be made righteous in Him before God.*
- *He became a curse so that you could be blessed.*
- *He carried your sickness so that you could be healed.*
- *He became poor that you might be made rich.*
- *He died your death so that you could live His life.*
- *He took on your human nature so that you could participate in His divine nature.*
- *He came to live in your home, the earth, so that you could live in His home, heaven.*
- *He became man, carried your sin, died and was buried, but He rose again to take mankind with Him into glory. Jesus is now seated at the right hand of the Father. He is interceding for you and representing mankind before God. He does this*

*so that the Holy Spirit will come to live in you
and represents the interests of the Father
through you. The moment that you acknowledge
your sin, repent and turn to Jesus, He comes
to dwell in your heart."*

PRESENTING THE PLAN OF SALVATION AND PRAYER

Once people are brought into the consolidation
room, the leader can present the plan of salvation.
He clearly and briefly explains the work of Christ
and the need to embrace it, using five foundational
points so that they can understand the decision
that they are making. See Matthew 13:19.

1.   ***God's love:***
     John 3:16, Jeremiah 31:3
2.   ***Sin:***
     Romans 3:23, 3:10-12
3.   ***Christ as the only Saviour:***
     John 14:6
4.   ***Repentance:***
     Acts 3:19, Romans 12:2
5.   ***Accepting (receiving) Jesus:***
     Revelation 3:20, John 1:12, Romans 10:9,10

Now pray the prayer of surrendering, emphasising
four things:

Their need of God: *"Lord, I need you"*.
Their state: *"Lord, I am a sinner"*.
Their repentance: *"Lord, forgive me"*.
Their surrender: *"Lord, I receive you"*.

Fill in the decision card.

It is extremely important to make a note of the needs
of the people who have just come to the Lord and to
pray for them. Pray for the new converts and their
needs. Ask if they would like to receive more information and help. Tell them also that someone will
contact them within the next few days.

Give them as a gift the booklet entitled "Encounter" and ask them to read 1 John once a day for the next seven days.

The transition between the first and second step in the Ladder of Success is almost automatic. Immediately after confessing Jesus as Lord the consolidation process begins there and then as the consolidator ministers to the new believer. Never forget to give them the "Encounter" pocket book. It is important and necessary for the new believer to take home something they can read to help them understand the decision they have made, and to strengthen their faith.

"Consolidation, An Effective Process for Making Disciples", by Claudia Fajardo.

the ladder of success
a practical guide

consolidate

CONSOLIDATE

You cannot enter the kingdom of God by human means, such as Christian tradition. You must be led personally to Christ and experience new birth by faith.

Paul said: *"For in Christ Jesus I have begotten you through the gospel" (1 Corinthians 4:15).*

James said, *"Of His own will He brought us forth by the word of truth, that we might be a kind of firstfruits of His creatures" (James 1:18).*

We can see from the verses above how the will of God operates though the preaching of the true Word and how it brings about conviction of sin, so that the new birth can be experienced.

The Apostle Paul won many people for the Lord at great personal cost. On many occasions he had to groan, shed tears and experience spiritual labour pains to ensure that they were properly born into new life. In *Galatians 4:19,* Paul aimed to make sure that each new convert would eventually reach the fullness of the stature of Christ.

The consolidation process begins immediately after the new believer has made his decision for Christ. The new believer is given an explanation of what has happened to re-affirm the redeeming work of Christ in his life.

Consolidation is *"the care and attention that we should give to every new believer in order to reproduce in him the character of Christ with the aim that he fulfils the purpose of God for his life which is to bear fruit that endures".*
The consolidation process was a practice of the early church: *"...strengthening the souls of the disciples,*

exhorting them to continue in the faith, and saying, 'We must through many tribulations enter the kingdom of God'" (Acts 14:22).

STARTING CONSOLIDATION

Encourage the new believer to live for Jesus. Take special care of him so he will not be discouraged or have any reason to backslide. The goal is to form the character of Jesus in the new disciple. Affirm him in his faith and build up a firm foundation for his full development as a fruitful leader, who in turn will be able to disciple others.

WHAT DOES IT COST TO CONSOLIDATE?

You need to give yourself totally to the formation of the new believer. This will demand love, dedication, effort and work. But we know that all this has its reward, and when we see people grow, we will be able to say, "It was worth it". We need to remember that the Lord Jesus commanded us to make disciples and that consolidation is the basic foundation for discipleship. A great example of what consolidation is all about is found in *Colossians 1:28-29: "Him we preach, warning every man and teaching every man in all wisdom, that we may present every man perfect in Christ Jesus. To this end I also labour, striving according to His working which works in me mightily."*

WHEN DOES THE CONSOLIDATION PROCESS BEGIN?

When the evangelism ends, take all the person's details. After you have returned home have a time of intercession and present yourself before God on behalf of the souls that have been entrusted to you. You cannot allow anyone who has made a decision for Christ to go without immediate help. The new believer needs to feel that he is important. Your dedication, love and interest will demonstrate to people how important they are.

WHERE DOES CONSOLIDATION TAKE PLACE?

Although personal assistance was given at the moment of commitment, it is the cell where the new disciple will be quickly consolidated. Invite the person you have won to take part in your cell.

As I have already emphasised, it is so important to understand the vision. We should first catch the vision in the spiritual realm, and then we will be able to understand its methodology. Each stage is an invitation to remain humble and to be constantly learning, so that we can faithfully transmit the vision to others.

CONSOLIDATION IN THE FIRST WEEK

PLACES FOR CONSOLIDATION

The success of the whole process depends on good consolidation. It is important to have a well-formed team to assist the new believers in their first week of Christian life.

Consolidation happens in two places:

A.   In the Cell

When the person makes a decision for Christ in the cell, the leader immediately starts the consolidation process. Together with his team, he is responsible for the consolidation.

B.   In the Church

When the decision is made in one of the church services, the process demands more co-ordination and hard work. It is necessary to have a team that has been specially trained to give first class assistance to the new convert. When the new believer starts to attend a cell, the cell leader becomes responsible for overseeing the process that will take the new believer to the School of Leaders - on the third step on the Ladder of Success.

THE DIRECTOR OF CONSOLIDATION

Because of the vital importance of consolidation, the ideal person responsible for its co-ordination is a pastor. This role will demand quite a lot of time. The Director of Consolidation should have a profound passion for the lost and an unshakeable love for new believers.

He is responsible for:

Recruiting *the consolidators*
Organising training
Directing *the prayer meetings and the planning and evaluation meetings*
Reviewing *the consolidation team's work from the previous week*
Raising *up a support team with representatives from each net.*

THE CONSOLIDATION TEAM

When the vision begins to be implemented in the church, the number of people involved in the first steps of the consolidation process will be small and the leader will have a great deal to do. It is necessary to invest heavily in the training of a group of volunteers. With a greater number of qualified people teams can take it in turns so that one group is not overloaded. It is also essential that you should find someone to work full-time in this area.

TRAINING THE TEAM

A. Recruiting
Call the cell leaders to an intensive consolidation training session. Show them the privilege of helping birth new people into the kingdom of God.

B. Training
Conduct lectures using the book *"Consolidation, An Effective Process for Making Disciples"*. These can be carried out during a Friday evening and Saturday.

C. Planning Rotas
Divide consolidators into teams depending on the number of people. Aim for twelve teams of consolidators, one for each month of the year. This is what happened with the priests in the Temple and with Solomon's managers.

D. Delegation
Tell them that they will be responsible for consolidating new believers from all the church services, until they hand them over into the hands of their "spiritual fathers". These cell leaders will then continue with the discipleship. Consolidators are responsible for using the four tools of consolidation:

1) *Personal contact*
2) *Telephone call*
3) *Personal visit*
4) *Placing in a cell*

the ladder of success a practical guide

THE ROLE OF THE TEAM

As we have already seen, the work of the Consolidation team begins at the moment of the altar call and ends when the person has been placed in a cell. For this, it is necessary to:

1. **Nominate the members of the team**
    Prepare the team that will be on duty during the month. Make a list of the people on duty for every month.

2. **Review**
    Go over the principles of consolidation with the group.

3. **Pray**
    Establish a weekly prayer time of at least two hours, when the whole group will engage in spiritual warfare, fast and pray for the decisions at each service and for the consolidation of the new believers.

4. **Assign tasks**
    Under the leader's co-ordination, the decision cards will be distributed among those who have become part of the Consolidation team.

Each one takes the following responsibilities:

- *Be ready at the moment of the altar call. Stay close to the platform to help the new believer.*
- *Accompany them to the consolidation room, according to the usual routine.*
- *Within forty-eight hours ring each person who has made a commitment.*
- *Visit the new person at his home within a week, no matter where he lives.*
- *Ensure that the new believer has been placed in a cell and is under a leader's care.*
- *The new believers can be placed in the cells of the actual consolidators on duty, if that is convenient.*

Consolidation should result in transformed life that can be reproduced in others.

The basis of consolidation is love and compassion for souls.

CONSOLIDATION PRINCIPLES

Verify the decision: Make sure that the information you are given is correct.

Teach the new believers: Take them through the Ladder of Success.

Fellowship: Introduce them to other believers, so that they can share with others.

Compassion: It is important that you empathise with them, remember you were once where they are now.

Attitude: Always be ready to help them in whatever they need.

Holiness: Remember that a new believer cannot see God, but will see God in what you do. Therefore you should always live a holy life.

Prayer: You are the model for the new believer and their goal will be to pray like you and as long as you do.

PLACEMENT

The decision cards are distributed among the team. The new believer should be placed in the cell nearest to their home.

Do not treat the decision cards lightly. They represent souls that we have to care for.

THE TELEPHONE CALL

- *Greet people.*
  Introduce yourself, give your name and explain the reason for your call.

- *Break the ice.*
  The best way to do this is by asking simple questions.

- *Start the conversation.*
  You could make a brief comment on how important it was for us to have him among our visitors.

- *Make an appointment for a visit.*
  This will be a great opportunity to share with other members of the family.

- *Pray.*
  Ask if they have any specific need, assuring him that God answers our prayers.

PREPARATION FOR THE VISIT

Analyse their problem

The decision card has a record of the specific needs of the person. Just like Jesus used a real need in the sinner to awaken his interest in spiritual matters (John 4), the best way to touch the people's hearts is to start from their point of need.

Ask God for a word

Talk to God about the new believer. Let God's love for him flood your heart. Turn your heart to the Holy Spirit and He will give you the appropriate word that will touch the person you are going to visit.

Choose an appropriate text

According to what the Holy Spirit places upon your heart, search in the Bible for an appropriate passage and meditate on it. One passage is enough. We should be simple, practical and objective in everything. Remember that the spiritual capacity of the new believer is still very limited.

Write the message

Organise your thoughts. It helps to write them down.
Write them again and again until there is a logical
sense and clarity in their presentation. Remember
that this is not a sermon but a brief message, which
should not exceed ten minutes.

Familiarise yourself with the message

Spend some time going over the written message,
so that you can present it in a natural tone of voice,
without having to read it.

Think about your appearance

Think of dressing appropriately, as a representative
of Christ. Avoid going to extremes and dress
for the situation. What is inside of you should be
reflected on the outside.

Be clean

Clean your teeth and have fresh breath. Your mouth
is the channel that delivers the Word of God. Be
careful about body odour. Keep your clothes clean.
Personal cleanliness should be the norm in the life
of a leader: *"And cleanse your bodies with
pure water ..."*.

Confirm the visit

Ring to confirm the date, the time and the place of
the visit as agreed during the previous telephone
call. Be polite and brief.

Meet up with your visitation partner

Meet with your visitation partner at an appropriate
place, pray together and ask God to use both of you
in a special way to touch the heart of the new believer. The goal is to make him a disciple of Christ and
this is only possible by the power of the Holy Spirit.
Your partner should be the one who is going to
come alongside the new believer as an elder brother
or a consolidator. Obviously he should be someone
that you are already training to become one of your
twelve.

Punctuality

Arrive on time. Let the new believer get used to
people who keep their word and who fulfil
what they say no matter what. Lateness is a big
character flaw.

Pray before going

Prayer is an indispensable tool every step of the way. Don't forget that before any spiritual project materialises on earth, it should first be generated by the prayers of the saints, moved by the Spirit of God and backed by His Word.

Dependence on the Holy Spirit

He is the one who convicts us and makes Jesus real in our experience. We are just His channels.

PURPOSES OF THE VISIT

Prayerfully prepare your message based on the needs of the new believer. Meet with your visitation companion and pray fervently for God's backing.

THE VISIT

When you visit a home you are bringing in the presence of Christ to that family, for it is as if Jesus Himself went there.

During your visit:

A. **Introduce yourself**
   It is fundamentally important that people know with whom they are dealing. Use a kind and sincere tone of voice.

B. **Open with prayer**
   Without giving the impression that you are some kind of mystic, briefly thank God for the opportunity to share with that precious family.

C. **Share a short portion of Scripture**
   It should bring hope to the needs of the family.

D. **Briefly explain the vision of the church**
   Explain about the net you represent. Be ready to listen to any suggestion they may have.

E. Pray
Pray for the needs of the people who are present. Do not feel afraid to ask for a supernatural miracle.

F. Release peace
At the end ask for the peace of Christ that surpasses all understanding to guard and protect all the members of that family.

Recommendations:

- Take care of your personal appearance.
- Talk and listen.
- Speak rather than preach.
- Do not go over the agreed time.
- Do not visit during meal times.

In case of objections:

- Don't be contentious.
- Be friendly with everyone.
- Be prepared to teach.
- Be gentle in correcting those who oppose you.
- Listen patiently.

READING
"Successful Leadership through the Goverment of 12" by Cesar Castellanos, Part 3, Chapter 9.

BASIC TEXT
"Consolidation, an Effective Process for Making Disciples" by Claudia Fajardo.

the ladder of success
a practical guide

PRE-ENCOUNTER

The new disciple is taken to the Pre-Encounter class, where he is prepared for the three-day Encounter. The Pre-Encounter is essential for the Encounter to be of maximum value and success.

Location: The class can take place in either the church or a cell.

Teachers: These can be pastors, G12 leaders or the cell leader.
When a church begins to implement the vision, the leadership is often loosely structured. This is why I suggest that the people leading the Pre-Encounters should be those who are more experienced biblically and spiritually, and clearly understand the vision.

Duration: One hour per week for four weeks, or two hours every two weeks. Obviously, everything depends on the needs of the person. If he is a new believer, it is important to consider time limits so that he can grow naturally.
The preparation for the Encounter starts as soon as the consolidation process begins. Participation in a class with other people, with someone who has more experience in teaching, is of great value.

Goal: To lead the new believer through basic steps of the Christian faith. The goal is to assure him of his salvation, explain the benefits of the cross and the power of God to deliver, and prepare the new believer for the Encounter.

We shall now look at guidelines for the preparation of those going to the Encounter.

Evangelistic Talk

THE FOUR SPIRITUAL LAWS

"But God demonstrates His own love toward us, in that while we were still sinners, Christ died for us" (Romans 5:8).

"But as many as received Him, to them He gave the right to become children of God, to those who believed in His name" (John 1:12).

Demonstrate the surpassing love of God for the lost to the person you are witnessing to and lead them to Christ.

INTRODUCTION

The whole universe is governed by laws. These laws were established by God to maintain the perfect order of the universe: *"...upholding all things by the word of His power" (Hebrews 1:3).*
Just as natural laws exist, so also do spiritual laws. Man has chosen to break them by his own will. This is why we need to know God's purpose for our lives.

GOD LOVES YOU AND HAS A MARVELLOUS PLAN FOR YOUR LIFE

"For God so loved the world that He gave His only begotten Son, that whoever believes in Him should not perish but have everlasting life" (John 3:16).

God hates sin, but loves the sinner. Man's disobedience separated him from the original purpose that God had planned for him. From a state of blessing, man found himself separated from God's glory. There was no other way to redeem mankind, except for the sacrificial offering provided by God. That offering had to be His own Son.

MAN IS SINFUL AND IS SEPARATED FROM GOD

We are aware that man has a nature that openly rebels against divine authority, giving honour rather to the appetites of the flesh. *"For all have sinned and fall short of the glory of God"* (Romans 3:23). This means that your immortal soul will be eternally separated from God and will go to a place of continuous torment, where there is no rest day or night.

JESUS CHRIST IS THE ONLY WAY TO SALVATION

Isaiah said: *"But He was wounded for our transgressions, He was bruised for our iniquities; the chastisement for our peace was upon Him, and by His stripes we are healed"* (Isaiah 53:5). Jesus willingly accepted our punishment in order to grant us complete redemption. *"For since by man came death, by Man also came the resurrection of the dead"* (1 Corinthians 15:21). *"Jesus said to him, 'I am the way, the truth and the life. No one comes to the Father except through Me'"* (John 14:6). Only through Jesus do we receive salvation and forgiveness of sins.

ACCEPTING JESUS CHRIST AS OUR LORD AND SAVIOUR

"But as many as received Him, to them He gave the right to become children of God, to those who believed in His name" (John 1:12). For a man to be reconciled to the Father, it is necessary to turn to Him, to surrender his will and to ask Jesus to come in and take control of His life. *"Behold, I stand at the door and knock. If anyone hears My voice and opens the door, I will come in to him and dine with him and he with Me"* (Revelation 3:20).

the ladder of success
a practical guide

CONCLUSION

All the punishment that we deserved as sinners fell on Jesus - the man who never committed any sin. All the good that Jesus deserved came to us simply by us believing in Him. God sees us through Jesus and we communicate with God through Him.

APPLICATION

After sharing these four spiritual laws, we should lead the person to give his life to Jesus. Then we guide him through the prayer of commitment.

Pre-Encounter Talk No. 1

THE NEW BIRTH

"Jesus answered and said to him, 'Most assuredly, I say to you, unless one is born again, he cannot see the kingdom of God'"
(John 3:3).

"Therefore, if anyone is in Christ, he is a new creation; old things have passed away; behold, all things have become new"
(2 Corinthians 5:17).

GOALS

To identify why the new birth is required.
Identify the advantages and results of the new birth.

INTRODUCTORY QUESTION

Do you think you have experienced the new birth?

INTRODUCTION

When we are born in the natural, God has already created within us our sex, skin pigmentation, height and weight, temperament, even some habits and desires. But to be born again means to acquire a spiritual life and mind that will become the mind of Christ.

For a long time people have looked for solutions to humanity's problems simply in social reform, forgetting that the root of every problem is in the spiritual realm. Once the spiritual problem has been solved, that will reflect in every area of people's lives.

The new birth is a creative act. God takes the believer's faith, and joins it to the power of the Holy Spirit. This produces the miracle of a new heart and spirit: "...*that which is born of the Spirit is spirit*" *(John 3:6).*

EVERYONE NEEDS A NEW BIRTH

"Who can say, 'I have kept my heart clean, I am pure from my sin?'" (Proverbs 20:9).

If Jesus had spoken to Zacchaeus a thief, or Mary Magdalene a sinner, or the thief who hung next to Him on the cross, saying, "He who is not born again cannot see the kingdom of God", one could easily understand that such bad people must change. However, it was not like this. He said this to Nicodemus, a teacher of the law, who prayed two hours a day, fasted twice a week and was zealous in Mosaic doctrine.
The idea that man is able to reform himself is, therefore, completely without foundation. The new birth is not an intellectual event, but it is a spiritual miracle.

WHO BRINGS ABOUT THE NEW BIRTH?

The Apostle James writes: "*Of His own will He brought us forth by the word of truth, that we might be a kind of first fruits of His creatures*" *(James 1:18).*

There is power in the Word of God. It has power to renew and to give life. It has power to resurrect and bring about deep and real changes in the life of a man. Jesus Christ said: "*and you will know the truth, and the truth will set you free.*" The truth is Jesus as He said of Himself : "*I am the way, the truth and the life.*"

John also taught:

"It is the Spirit who gives life; the flesh profits nothing. The words that I have speak to you are spirit, and they are life" (John 6:63).

The new birth can only happen by receiving the Holy Spirit. In order to receive Him you need to die to sin. The Holy Spirit is holy and He will only live in a life that has been regenerated by the blood of Jesus.

The prophet Ezekiel said, *"I will give you a new heart and put a new spirit within you; I will take the heart of stone out of your flesh and give you a heart of flesh. I will put My Spirit in you and cause you to walk in My statutes, and you will keep My laws and judgements and do them" (Ezekiel 36:26-27).*

This new birth comes directly from the Holy Spirit, who through faith releases the spirit of life into the new believer.

ADVANTAGES OF THE NEW BIRTH

Only the spiritual man can see the kingdom of God. His spiritual eyes are opened, and he can perceive all the things that are hidden to the natural man. Paul said: *"Eye has not seen, nor ear heard, nor have entered the heart of man, the things which God has prepared for those who love him" (1 Corinthians 2:9).*

We can summarise the advantages of the new birth as following:

1. **Spiritual eyes are opened.** Sin blinds the eyes, but when we accept Jesus, our spiritual eyes are opened.

2. **Moving from darkness into light.** Sin takes us through dark paths. Conversion makes us turn our backs on darkness and directs our steps onto a new way, the path of light.

3. **Conversion from Satan's dominion to God's.** Sin enslaved us, keeping us under Satan's dominion. When we were converted to Christ, we came under the government of God.

4. **Through faith in Jesus we receive pardon for sin.** Faith believes that our sins deserve punishment, but that Jesus carried them in His body.

5. **We receive an inheritance with the saints.** Paul said: *"He who did not spare His own Son, but gave Him up for us, how will He not also give everything to us? (Romans 8:32).*

CONCLUSION

No matter what his current moral state, every person needs a new birth. We cannot change ourselves. The new birth is produced through the Word and the Holy Spirit.

Only through the new birth can a person receive his spiritual sight and move from darkness into light and from sin to holiness.

The new birth comes through faith. We should receive the revelation of the new man and of the death of the old man.

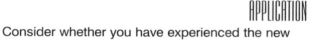

APPLICATION

Consider whether you have experienced the new birth.

Considering the advantages of the new birth, evaluate whether you have received and experienced the benefits set apart for the new believer.

Consider the importance of the sacrifice of Jesus on the cross of Calvary. If God gave Jesus to redeem us from our sins, how much more will He give to us?

"What then shall we say to these things? If God is for us, who can be against us? He who did not spare His own Son, but delivered Him up for us all, how shall He not with Him also freely give us all things?" (Romans 8:31-32).

the ladder of success
a practical guide

Pre-Encounter Talk No. 2

PRINCIPLES OF DELIVERANCE

"Then Jesus said to those Jews who believed in Him 'If you abide in My word, you are My disciples indeed. And you shall know the truth, and the truth shall make you free"'
(John 8:31-32).

GOALS

To give the basic principles for deliverance from different kind of bondages that may exist in the new believer's life. During the Encounter there will be ministry time in these areas, and if people have the right response and attitude, a miracle will take place.

The work of Christ when He came to the world - to die, to be buried and to rise again - was at very high price. We can be sure that whoever believes in Him will experience deep deliverance from any kind of demonic power or influence. *"The Spirit of the Lord God is upon Me, because the Lord has anointed Me to preach good tidings to the poor; He has sent Me to heal the brokenhearted, to proclaim liberty to the captives, and the opening of the prison to those who are bound" (Isaiah 61:1).*

The deliverance is complete when the person feels that the oppression of past curses no longer holds him, when vices do not dominate him, when there is deliverance from the sin of his forefathers, and when he feels that the fullness of God is flowing freely through his life.

THE CONDITION OF A SINNER

Man rebelled against God and became involved in all kinds of evil. All these things brought consequences for man. He began experiencing all kinds of curses, in such a way that the enemy built up strongholds around him, bound him, oppressed him and enslaved him. Because of sin Satan found a legal right to rule man and enslave him.

Sin separated mankind from God.

Jesus answered them, *"Most assuredly I say to you, whoever commits sin is a slave of sin" (John 8:34).*

The world, with all its deceit and destructive values, leaves a great emptiness in the soul of man.

"For all that is in the world - the lust of the flesh, the lust of the eyes, and the pride of life - is not of the Father but is of the world. And the world is passing away, but he who does the will of God lives forever" (1 John 2:16,17).

The pleasures of the flesh with all its vices not only corrupt the mind, but also weaken one's health, provoking all types of sicknesses and cutting short one's life.

"And those who are Christ's have crucified the flesh with its passions and desires" (Galatians 5:24).

"The works of the flesh are evident, which are: adultery, fornication, uncleanness, lewdness, idolatry, sorcery, hatred, contentions, jealousy, outbursts of wrath, selfish ambitions, dissensions, heresies, envy, murders, drunkenness, revelries, and the like; of which I tell you beforehand, just as I told you in time past, that those who practise such things will not inherit the kingdom of God" (Galatians 5: 19-21).

The Devil brings all kinds of bondages into the life of the sinner. *"In this the children of God and the children of the devil are manifest: Whoever does not practise righteousness is not of God, nor is he who does not love his brother" (1 John 3:10).*

And the Lord, rebuking the religious leaders of His time who were acting with a hypocritical attitude, told them, *"You are of your father the devil, and the desires of your father you want to do. He was a murderer from the beginning, and does not stand in the truth, because there is no truth in him. When he speaks a lie, he speaks from his own resources, for he is a liar, and the father of it"* (John 8:44).

When someone allows sin in his life, bondages, curses, and strongholds will arise, affecting the whole human life: *"...may your whole spirit, soul and body be preserved blameless at the coming of our Lord Jesus Christ."* 1 Thessalonians 5:23 shows three areas that the enemy tries to control, dominate and enslave.

These bondages can take hold of people:

1. Spiritual - *blinding and keeping them in darkness. This makes people surrender to sins of idolatry and to the practice of witchcraft. Man thinks he is serving God and does not realise that he is actually displeasing Him. "In whom the god of this world hath blinded the minds of them which believe not, lest the light of the glorious gospel of Christ, who is the image of God, should shine unto them"* (2 Corinthians 4:4).

2. Soulish - *the worst wounds that mankind suffer are afflicted in the soul and their main cause is rejection. Jesus suffered rejection on the cross of Calvary, so that we would be accepted by God through Him. Only through Jesus can the soul's wounds be healed.*

3. Physical - *the enemy has attacked mankind with all types of sicknesses and deformities. Whoever rejects God exposes himself to suffer the consequences of sin with all kinds of sicknesses and curses.*

4. Financial - with poverty and ruin. Moses said: *"...And you will grope at noonday, as a blind man gropes in darkness; you shall not prosper in your ways; you shall be only oppressed and plundered continually, and no one shall save you ... Your ox shall be slaughtered before your eyes, but you shall not eat of it; your donkey shall be taken away from before you and shall not be restored to you; your sheep shall be given to your enemies, and you shall have no one to rescue them"* (Deuteronomy 28:29, 31) .

THE PROVISION OF GOD FOR OUR DELIVERANCE

We are freed by the power of the cross. Jesus brought all our curses to it, as it is written in *Galatians 3:13: "Christ has redeemed us from the curse of the law, having become a curse for us (for it is written, 'Cursed is everyone who hangs on a tree')"*. On the cross He reversed the curse and has now the right to deliver us. We do not speak about the cross itself, but what the work on Calvary represents. The death of Christ became our death. It is there that all our debts were cancelled. All the rage and anger of Satan was crushed by the power of Jesus. The cross became the mortal weapon against our adversary and the kingdom of darkness. The cross alone can set man free from slavery to sin, Satan's oppression and the consequences of the curse. The cross sets man free and enables him to walk the path of blessing. Paul said: *"For the message of the cross is foolishness to those who are perishing, but to us who are being saved it is the power of God"* (1 Corinthians 1:18). Verse 21 adds: *"For since, in the wisdom of God, the world through wisdom did not know God, it pleased God through the foolishness of the message preached to save those who believe."* Then verse 23: *"but we preach Christ crucified, to the Jews a stumbling block and to the Greeks foolishness."*

the ladder of success
a practical guide

The cross delivers us from:

- Sin - *Romans 6:23: "For the wages of sin is death; but the gift of God is eternal life through Jesus Christ our Lord."*

- Demonic bondages - Luke declares *"how God anointed Jesus of Nazareth with the Holy Spirit and with power, and who went around doing good and healing all who were oppressed by the devil, for God was with Him" (Acts 10:38).*

- Ruin - the psalmist declares that God *"sent His word and healed them, and delivered them from their destructions" (Psalm 107:20).*

- Affliction - Isaiah 63:9 says: *"In all their affliction He was afflicted, and the angel of His presence saved them: in His love and in His pity He redeemed them; and He bore them, and carried them all the days of old."*

PREPARING FOR DELIVERANCE

a. *Desire to live in freedom.* God is willing to deliver us. He gave us the means to be delivered in Christ, but man has to desire it with his own will. *Matthew 11:28-30 says: "Come to Me, all you who labour and are heavy laden, and I will give you rest. Take My yoke upon you and learn from Me, for I am gentle and lowly in heart, and you will find rest for your souls. For My yoke is easy and My burden is light."*

b. *Identify the causes for the bondages.* Psalm *139:23,24 says: "Search me, O God, and know my heart; Try me, and know my anxieties; See if there is any wicked way in me; And lead me in the way everlasting."*

c. *Repentance and confession of sins.* Deliverance is not a substitute for repentance. Because of sin, Satan has legal rights. Those legal rights will only be made void by repentance and when the person renounces his sinful life. *"I tell you, no; but unless you repent you will all likewise perish" (Luke 13:3).*

d. *Faith.* Hebrews *11:6* says: *"But without faith it is impossible to please Him, for he who comes to God must believe that He is, and that He is a rewarder of those who diligently seek Him."*

e. *Take hold of the truth. "Therefore if the Son makes you free, you shall be free indeed" (John 8:36).*

f. *Prayer and fasting. "However, this kind does not go out except by prayer and fasting" (Matthew 17:21).*

APPLICATION

Pray with the new believer using the steps given above. During the Pre-Encounter sessions, encourage them to register for the Encounter. If they are willing, their lives will be completely transformed.

the ladder of success
a practical guide

Pre-Encounter Talk No. 3

THE ASSURANCE OF SALVATION

"For God so loved the world that He gave His only begotten Son, that whoever believes in Him should not perish but have everlasting life. For God did not send His Son into the world to condemn the world, but that the world through Him might be saved" *(John 3:16-17).*

GOALS

For the new believer to experience assurance of salvation through the work of Jesus on the cross.

INTRODUCTORY QUESTIONS

There are two frequently used questions in "Evangelism Explosion":

1) If you were to die right now where would you spend eternity?

The next question follows on from the reply to the first:

2) Supposing you arrive at the gates of heaven, what would you say to God if He asked you: Why should I let you in?

IMPLICATIONS OF THE PLAN OF SALVATION

God's plan for salvation has the following aspects: Justification, regeneration, sanctification and redemption.

JUSTIFICATION

Justification means to 'declare righteous'. This is the act through which God declares that the sinner who believes in Jesus, and confesses his faith in Him and His work, is just and acceptable in His sight: *"Being justified freely by His grace through the redemption that is in Christ Jesus" (Romans 3:24).*

SANCTIFICATION

To be sanctified means to be holy and set apart for God. A person becomes holy through grace. Sanctification is consecration fully to God both in the moral and in the spiritual realm. Holiness is produced in the believer by the work of the Holy Spirit: *"Now may the God of peace Himself sanctify you completely; and may your whole spirit, soul and body be preserved blameless at the coming of our Lord Jesus Christ" (1 Thessalonians 5:23).*

REGENERATION

Regeneration means we change our way of thinking in relation to sin. Our mind becomes open to everything relating to God, especially to the incarnation of His Son and His redeeming work. It is the Holy Spirit who permits this regeneration in the inner man both morally and spiritually: *"But the natural man does not receive the things of the Spirit of God, for they are foolishness to him; nor can he know them, because they are spiritually discerned" (1 Corinthians 2:14).*

REDEMPTION

Salvation is directly associated with the redemption of man, and this redemption is likened to someone paying a ransom for a slave. Because there was no one on earth able to pay the price to ransom (redeem) mankind from his sins, God sent His only Son to do it, delivering mankind from eternal

the ladder of success
a practical guide

condemnation: *"But God demonstrates His own love toward us, in that while we were still sinners, Christ died for us" (Romans 5:8).*

Paul said: *"In Him we have redemption through His blood, the forgiveness of sins, according to the riches of His grace" (Ephesians 1:7).*

GOD'S PROMISES FOR YOU

Eternal life
"Most assuredly, I say to you, he that believes in Me has everlasting life. I am the bread of life. Your fathers ate the manna in the wilderness, and are dead. This is the bread which comes down from heaven, that one may eat of it and not die. I am the living bread which came down from heaven. If anyone eats of this bread, he will live forever; and the bread that I will give is My flesh, which I shall give for the life of the world" (John 6:47-51).

Forgiveness of sin
"If we say that we have no sin, we deceive ourselves, and the truth is not in us. If we confess our sins, He is faithful and just to forgive us our sins, and to cleanse us from all unrighteousness. If we say that we have not sinned, we make Him a liar, and His word is not in us" (1 John 1:8-10).

Position of a son:
"But as many as received Him, to them gave He the right to become children of God, to those who believed in His name" (John 1:12).

Inheritance with Christ
"And if children, then heirs - heirs of God and joint heirs with Christ, if indeed we suffer with Him, that we may also be glorified together" (Romans 8:17).

Things that you should know regarding:

The new nature
"Therefore if anyone is in Christ, he is a new creation; old things have passed away; behold, all things have become new" (2 Corinthians 5:17).

The inner witness
"For you did not receive the spirit of bondage again to fear, but you received the Spirit of adoption by whom we cry out, 'Abba, Father'. The Spirit Himself bears witness with our spirit that we are children of God" (Romans 8:15-16).

What your life will begin to display:

A hunger for studying the Bible
"As newborn babes, desire the pure milk of the word, that ye may grow thereby" (1 Peter 2:2).

Holiness
"But as He who called you is holy, so you also be holy in all your conduct, because it is written, 'Be holy, for I am holy'" (1 Peter 1:15-16).

Love for the brethren
"We know that we have passed from death to life, because we love the brethren. He who does not love his brother abides in death" (1 John 3:14).

Unceasing witness
"For we cannot but speak the things which we have seen and heard" (Acts 4:20).

FINAL QUESTIONS

According to Galatians 3:13, from what did Jesus redeem us when He died crucified on the cross?

APPLICATION

Examine your whole life and see if there is any area of sin that you have not confessed to God. Renounce it and begin to enjoy the sanctification that comes with salvation.

Pre-Encounter Talk No. 4

THE POWER OF THE SCRIPTURES

"All scripture is given by inspiration of God, and is profitable for doctrine, for reproof, for correction, for instruction in righteousness, that the man of God may be complete, thoroughly equipped for every good work" (2 Timothy 3:16-17).

Verse to memorise

"But everyone who hears these sayings of Mine, and does not do them, will be like a foolish man who built his house on sand: and the rain descended, the floods came, and the winds blew and beat on that house; and it fell. And great was its fall" (Matthew 7: 26-27).

GOALS

For the new believer to experience the power of the Word of God.
To keep the Word in their heart and be able to put it into practice.

INTRODUCTORY QUESTION

What steps should be considered to enable you to hear the voice of God?

"Now it shall come to pass, if you diligently obey the voice of the Lord your God, to observe carefully all His commandments which I command you today, that the Lord your God will set you high above all nations of the earth. And all these blessings shall come upon you and overtake you, because you obey the voice of the Lord your God" (Deuteronomy 28:1-2).

INTRODUCTION

We should love the Word and follow its instructions as the captain of a ship adheres to his compass. The Bible is a great treasure as it contains the answer to all our needs.

WHAT IS THE BIBLE?

The word Bible comes from the Greek terms *"biblos"* and *"biblion"* (in the diminutive form) which both mean "book". *"Then said Jesus to those Jews who believed Him, 'If you abide in My word, you are my disciples indeed. And you shall know the truth, and the truth shall make you free.'" (John 8:31-32)*

IMPORTANCE OF THE BIBLE

Apart from having power to transform lives, the Bible also stands out because:

- It is God's Word and the revelation of Christ.
  "Now then, we are ambassadors for Christ, as though God were pleading through us: we implore you on Christ's behalf, be reconciled to God" (2 Corinthians 5:20).

- It contains the divine laws.
  "But this is the covenant that I will make with the house of Israel after those days, says the Lord: I will put My law in their minds, and write it on their hearts; and I will be their God, and they shall be My people. No more shall every man teach his neighbour, and every man his brother, saying, 'Know the Lord,' for they shall all know Me, from the least of them to the greatest of them, says the Lord. For I will forgive their iniquity, and their sin I will remember no more" (Jeremiah 31:33-34).

- Its content, in 66 books, summarises the work of about 40 writers from different periods.

the ladder of success a practical guide

Jesus said: *"Heaven and earth will pass away, but My words will by no means pass away"* (Matthew 24:35).

Isaiah prophesied: *"The grass withers, the flower fades, but the word of our God stands for ever"* (Isaiah 40:8).

Things that make the Bible unique:

- The Bible is the revelation of God to mankind. 2 Peter 1:20-21 says: *"Above all, you must understand that no prophecy of Scripture came about by the prophet's own interpretation. For prophecy never had its origin in the will of man, but men spoke from God as they were carried along by the Holy Spirit"*.

- It refers to the salvation of mankind. *"Then Jesus said to them, 'Most assuredly, I say unto you, Moses did not give you the bread from heaven, but My Father gives you the true bread from heaven. For the bread of God is He who comes down from heaven and gives life to the world'"* (John 6:32-33).

- It refers to the truth. *"I have not written to you because you do not know the truth, but because you know it, and that no lie is of the truth"* (1 John 2:21).

- Jesus is the central character. *"Philip said to him, 'Lord, show us the Father, and it is sufficient for us.' Jesus said to him, 'Have I been with you so long, and yet you have not known Me, Philip? He who has seen Me has seen the Father; so how can you say, 'Show us the Father?'"* (John 14:8-9).

HOW TO DRAW NEAR TO THE WORD

1. Listen carefully to the voice of God on a daily basis.
   "Now it shall come to pass, if you diligently obey the voice of the Lord your God, to observe carefully all His commandments which I command you today, that the Lord your God will set you high above all nations of the earth. And all these blessings shall come upon you and overtake you, because you obey the voice of the Lord your God" (Deuteronomy 28:1-2).

2. Read it with a right attitude.

3. Meditate on it (undertake detailed study).
   "You search the Scriptures, for in them you think you have eternal life; and these are they which testify of Me" (John 5:39).

4. Put its commands into practice.
   "Your word is a lamp to my feet, and a light to my path" (Psalm 119:105).

5. Communicate it and confess it.
   "For with the heart one believes unto righteousness, and with the mouth confession is made unto salvation" (Romans 10:10).

HOW TO STUDY THE WORD

A. Choose an appropriate place.
B. Make studying a habit.
C. Keep a devotional notebook in which you write every day:

> Message from God for me today
> The promise of God for my life
> The command to obey
> Personal application
> Scripture verse to memorise

the ladder of success
a practical guide

BENEFITS OF DRAWING NEAR TO THE WORD

- *It teaches (doctrine)*
- *It convicts (makes us aware of our pitfalls)*
- *It corrects (lead us to the right path)*
- *It instructs (shapes our character)*

HOW DO I OBTAIN THAT POWER FOR MY LIFE?

Set apart fifteen minutes a day to do as follows:

- 5 minutes to speak with God.
- 5 minutes to read the Bible, starting with the Gospel of John and finishing with Revelation.
- 5 minutes to meditate on what you have read.

If we discover the secret of living in communion with God, we will find 'heaven's treasure'.

FINAL QUESTION

What are the benefits for the person who draws near to the Word?

APPLICATION

Determine to maintain a real relationship with God through regular daily Bible study. Determine to read a set number of chapters every day and memorise the texts God uses to speak to you directly. Start with the Gospel of John.

THE ENCOUNTER

WHAT IS AN ENCOUNTER?

An encounter with Jesus is the most beautiful experience any human being can have. When God created human beings He left an empty place in their hearts so that man would seek for his happiness to be complete. That emptiness can only be filled through the Lord Jesus Christ. The patriarch Job exclaimed *"Oh, that I knew where I might find Him, that I might come to His seat! I would present my case before him" (Job 23:3-4).* The Encounter is the first experience of coming face to face with God and His Word. It also confronts you and your past and uproots its negative influences totally from your life. You will be able to reflect on your daily life and in faith plan for a better future.

GENERAL GOALS

The Bible, teaching, ministry, workshops and videos will help the new believer to:

- *Be sure of his salvation.*
- *Experience genuine repentance.*
- *Break chains that bind him to the past.*
- *Receive emotional (inner) healing.*
- *Receive and experience the fullness of the Holy Spirit.*
- *Have clarity regarding the vision.*

the ladder of success
a practical guide

THE ORGANISATION

WHERE SHOULD THE ENCOUNTER BE CARRIED OUT?

It is preferable to be away from the city. If that is not possible, it could be in the city at a venue where people can spend three uninterrupted days together. It could be in a conference centre, hotel or leisure centre.

PARTICIPANTS

Only those who have gone through the Pre-Encounter should take part. The group should be homogeneous – men, women, young men or young women or married couples. Boys and girls can participate together in the Children's Encounters.

COST

The price fixed to cover the Encounter expenses. The disciple should pay his own costs.

DURATION

They generally take place at weekends, beginning on Friday evening, continuing all day Saturday and finishing sometime on Sunday afternoon.

SIZE OF THE GROUP

We aim for each of the twelve to take approximately six people to the Encounter making an average of seventy-two people. The co-ordinator will have twelve guides to help with the ministry. Every guide should make sure that every participant is fully ministered to. That way one guide is not overloaded.

TEAM

The team consists of a spiritual guide, a co-ordinator and a group of guides. The team should have been trained in the different ministries during the previous one or two months.

THE TOPICS

Encounters are for homogeneous groups, therefore the topics are prepared according to the needs of each group. A large part of the basic material can be found in the series *"As Firm as the Rock"*.

REQUIREMENTS

The Encounter is residential; no one may leave before it ends. Each person attending should fill in a registration form, complete the Pre-Encounter, and arrive well prepared and with an open heart.

TEAM FUNCTIONS AND RESPONSIBILITIES

SPIRITUAL GUIDE

Cares for the spiritual well-being of the team during the preparation as well as during the actual Encounter. The spiritual guide should also:

- *Minister to the team.*
- *Go over the lectures assigned to the guides.*
- *Promote team-work.*
- *Minister at the main lectures during the Encounter, such as: Deliverance, Inner Healing and Repentance.*

CO-ORDINATOR

Co-ordinates every activity within the Encounter, at both the spiritual and administrative levels:

On a spiritual level the co-ordinator:

A. *Prepares the spiritual atmosphere of the Encounter through his own personal efforts and those of the team.*

B. *Asks God for a specific word for the Encounter and then shares it with the team. This is essential, because through prayer God will give a Rhema word and reveal His specific plan for people in each particular Encounter.*

C. *Encourages and guides the team in prayer, fasting and spiritual warfare for the Encounter.*

D. *Through prayer, watches over the unity and holiness of the team and its sensitivity to the Holy Spirit.*

E. *Motivates the team to pray on a daily basis for the Encounter and engage in spiritual warfare against any opposition that may arise before or during the Encounter.*

F. *Organises a prayer and fasting chain during the preparation for the Encounter.*

G. *Supervises and evaluates the Encounter, ensuring that all the goals have been met.*

H. *Ministers the Post-Encounter in order to support and strengthen all the teaching received in the Encounter and continues to oversee the development of each person who attended the Encounter.*

On an administrative level the co-ordinator:

1. *Plans, organises and supervises the actual activity of the Encounter, delegating duties to each guide.*

2. *Ensures that the preparation is done.*

3. *Allocates the groups of people and evaluates whether each person who attends has been discipled properly.*

4. *Chooses an intercession team for the preparation and development of the Encounter.*

5. *Delegates lectures to the guides, then supervises and evaluates the fulfilment of goals for each lecture.*

GUIDES

- *Need to be extremely familiar with the Encounter material.*
- *Aim to take between six to ten people to the Encounter.*
- *Learn, study and know the lectures which they have been allocated.*
- *Prepare themselves by prayer and fasting.*
- *Communicate with their designated group during and after the Encounter.*
- *Seek unity and interaction with the other guides, having a humble spirit and a servant heart, always being polite and pleasant, prudent in words and with a Christian attitude.*
- *Disciple each one of the people they have invited.*
- *Ensure that after the Encounter and Post-Encounter, every person is placed in a cell, goes to the School of Leaders, and is being discipled by a G12 leader, starting on the Ladder of Success, and on their way to becoming a leader in their own right.*

the ladder of success

a practical guide

PREPARATION OF THE TEAM FOR THE ENCOUNTER

ORDER OF ACTIVITIES

Suggestions for effective time management during the preparation for the Encounter:

1st Meeting. Talk: *'The Privilege of the Call'* (with ministry time). The co-ordinator should share with the team of guides the prophetic word for the Encounter. Plan a rota of prayer and fasting with the whole team.

2nd Meeting. Introduction of the team. (The guides' testimony).

3rd Meeting. Talk: *'Keeping ourselves in total holiness'* (with ministry time). The guides share any word for the Encounter that God may have given them during that week. Define the specific goals with the team, followed by prayer and spiritual warfare for the Encounter.

4th Meeting. Talk: *'What it is to be a guide'* (with ministry time). Delegate responsibilities, assign each Encounter lecture to the appropriate guide and explain its goals.

5th Meeting. Talk: *'Having a heart full of love and compassion'* (with ministry time). Intercessory prayer for any specific areas God may have revealed.

6th Meeting. Go over the outlines of the lectures they have been assigned, pray for the Encounter.

7th Meeting. Go over the complete lectures. Check over the delegated responsibilities.

8th   Meeting. Talk: *'Depending on the Holy Spirit'* (with ministry time). Final corrections to the lectures (by the spiritual guide).

9th   Meeting. Spiritual warfare for each lecture and specific areas of the whole Encounter.

10th Meeting. Ministry time with the spiritual guide.

11th Meeting. Preliminary meeting with the participants to verify their preparation.

12th Meeting. Final meeting with all the participants and their families for prayer and spiritual warfare.

We will now look at the outlines of each of the preparation lectures for the team. These are extracted from the Youth Net Encounter Manual.

Team Preparation Talk No. 1

THE PRIVILEGE OF THE CALL

"Now the Lord said to Abram: 'Get out of your country, from your family and from your father's house, to a land that I will show you. And I will make you a great nation; and I will bless you, and make your name great; and you shall be a blessing. And I will bless those who bless you, and I will curse him who curses you; and in you all the families of the earth shall be blessed'" (Genesis 12:1-3).

Verse to memorise
"And I will make you a great nation; and I will bless you, and make your name great; and you shall be a blessing" (Genesis 12:2).

GOALS

To make the guides understand the importance of their responsibility, so that they are successful in their task.

INTRODUCTORY QUESTIONS

Are you sure of your calling?
A calling is a gift from God for each one of His children. Abraham was not seeking a call, but it pleased God to reveal Himself to him and to call him.

RESPONDING TO THE CALL

Though the call to Abraham came directly from God, it was up to him to believe it, obey it and respond to it.

We find some interesting aspects in Abraham's life about how he responded to the call.

1. *Immediate obedience. He did not wait for weeks or months, but he immediately responded to the divine call.*
2. *Total obedience. Abraham obeyed every word that the Lord revealed to him.*
3. *Genuine faith. The faith of Abraham was as pure as a child's: he never doubted any of the words God gave him.*
4. *Perseverance. Abraham did not look at the circumstances, but believed that God would be faithful in what He had promised to do.*

BENEFITS OF RESPONDING TO THE CALL

It pleases God. God was so pleased with Abraham's response to each one of the tests that He put him through, that He established an intimate relationship with him.

It made the promise of God real in his life.

Abraham became a friend of God. God established His covenant with him and all his descendants. He then received the anointing for multiplication. (*Genesis 17:1-6*).

CONCLUSION

Just as Abraham believed Jehovah and it was counted to him for righteousness so every guide should believe God, be sure of his calling and respond faithfully to it.

APPLICATION

Minister to the guides, leading them through every point explained above, and encouraging them to value and take up their calling to lead the people of God.

Team Preparation Talk No. 2

HOLINESS, THE KEY TO OBTAINING GOD'S BACKING

"To grant us that we, being delivered from the hand of our enemies, might serve Him without fear, in holiness and righteousness before Him, all the days of our life" (Luke 1:74-75).

GOALS

To teach every guide to value holiness and to remain holy as a key to seeing God's power in their lives.

INTRODUCTORY QUESTION

What benefits does a holy life bring?

To be holy is to have been chosen and set apart by God before the foundation of the world. God chose us for His service and He does not share us with anything or anyone.

The benefit that a holy life brings is that God will be able to use you. In Judges 13:25 God sanctified Samson that he would be full of the Spirit of God, enabling him to deliver the people of Israel.

CHARACTERISTICS OF A LEADER

1. *Is chosen by God in times of crisis*
2. *Is given supernatural strength*
3. *Boundaries are set to maintain his integrity*
4. *Is given the task of bringing freedom to the people of Israel*

WHAT CAN TAKE AWAY OUR HOLINESS?

1. *Confidence in the flesh*
2. *Playing with temptation*
3. *Excessive self-confidence*
4. *Being unequally yoked with an unbeliever*
5. *Giving in to pressure from other people*
   See Judges 15 and 16.

CONSEQUENCES OF LOSING ONE'S HOLINESS

- *You become a slave of your enemies*
- *You completely lose the vision of God*
- *You are mocked and ridiculed*
- *You suffer slander and are treated badly*
- *You die*

HOW IS HOLINESS RESTORED?

1. *Repent*
2. *Plead for God's favour*
3. *Ask for the renewal of the anointing*
4. *Commit to accomplish your task faithfully*

CONCLUSION

Samson, though he was the strongest man in the world, did not care about his relationship with God, and this brought his destruction. Every believer, no matter how strong spiritually, exposes himself to the same potential disaster as Samson if he is not careful to continually walk with God.

APPLICATION

During the ministry time we should lead the guides to examine themselves, to recognise their failures, and in a simple way ask the Lord to forgive, restore and renew their relationship with Him.

the ladder of success
a practical guide

Team Preparation Talk No. 3

WHAT DOES IT MEAN TO BE A GUIDE?

*"The righteous should choose his friends carefully,
for the way of the wicked leads them astray"
(Proverbs 12:26).*

Verse to memorise
*" For as many as are led by the Spirit of God, these
are sons of God" (Romans 8:14).*

GOALS

To motivate the guide to carry out his task with all
the diligence that the work of God demands.

INTRODUCTORY QUESTION

What does it mean to be a guide?
*"However, when He, the Spirit of truth, has come,
He will guide you into all truth; for He will not speak
on His own authority, but whatever He hears He will
speak; and He will tell you things to come"
(John 16:13).*

To be a guide is to be a representative of Jesus on
earth. It is to communicate faithfully the message
that has been assigned, to be a watchman and
warn concerning the future. It means to be a person under authority. *As Romans 13:1 says: "Let
every soul be subject to the governing authorities. For
there is no authority except from God, and the authorities that exist are appointed by God."*

IMPORTANCE OF THE PREPARATION

A guide should be well balanced and properly prepared.

On a spiritual level he should know the Bible and study it in depth. He should have a strong relationship with God through prayer and fasting.

On a personal level he should excel in everything he does and promote unity within the team.

THE GUIDE'S ATTITUDE

- The correct attitude always comes as a result of being in God's presence.
- The guide has a humble and serving attitude. *"For even the Son of Man did not come to be served, but to serve, and to give His life a ransom for many" (Mark 10:45).*
- He allows God to take and mould his life.
- He has authority because of the transparency of his ways.
- He treats everyone equally, with no preferences.
- He identifies himself with the suffering of other people.

CONCLUSION

The guide's work should be done with excellence and discipline, as it will help the spiritual growth of those who attend the Encounter.

APPLICATION

During the ministry time lead the guides to reflect on every aspect of this teaching and lead them into a radical commitment to serve with excellence.

the ladder of success — a practical guide

Team Preparation Talk No. 4

CHARACTERISTICS OF A HEART PLEASING TO GOD

"Greater love has no one than this, than to lay down his life for his friends" (John 15:13).

Verse to memorise
"And when Jesus went out He saw a great multitude; and He was moved with compassion for them and healed their sick" (Matthew 14:14).

GOALS

To make the guide understand the importance of knowing the desire of God's heart, which is to save the lost because of His great love and compassion.

INTRODUCTORY QUESTION

What is love with compassion?

INTRODUCTION

Jesus gave us the example of real love by giving His life in our place, showing God's love for humanity through the cross.
God gives all His love without reservation.
According to Matthew 14:14, Jesus had compassion on the multitudes, He understood their needs and made every effort to meet them.
Compassion makes us like Jesus who has compassion for people and meets their needs.

WHY SHOULD WE HAVE LOVE AND COMPASSION?

It is the desire of God's heart.
"So I sought for a man among them that should make a wall, and stand in the gap before Me on behalf of the land, that I should not destroy it; but I found no one" (Ezekiel 22:30).

It is a commandment.
"These things I command you, that you love one another" (John 15:17).

HOW DO WE EXPRESS LOVE AND COMPASSION?

- Understanding man's condition without God.
- Putting ourselves in someone else's place.
- Feeling a burden for the needs of another.
- Crying out with all our heart for mercy.

As the prophet Daniel did - in Daniel 9 - when he turned to God in prayer and supplication, identifying with the sins of the people, as if he had sinned, and then confessing them before God, and pleading for forgiveness, favour and divine mercy.

CONCLUSION

Jesus gave us our example of the greatest love and compassion. These were the reasons why He came into the world. In the same way, we should make every effort to follow Him and fulfil His commandments.

APPLICATION

During the ministry time, acknowledge the hardness in our hearts to the needs of others and ask for real love and divine compassion.

the ladder of success

a practical guide

Team Preparation Talk No. 5

DEPENDING ON THE HOLY SPIRIT

"Then the Spirit of the Lord will come upon you, and you will prophesy with them and be turned into another man"
(1 Samuel 10:6).

GOAL

To teach every guide to depend completely on the Holy Spirit for every task that is assigned to them.

INTRODUCTORY QUESTION

What does it mean to depend on the Holy Spirit?

To depend on the Holy Spirit means:
1. *To trust and be dependent totally on Him*
2. *Complete surrender of our life*
3. *Being sensitive to His voice*
4. *Immediate obedience*

HOW TO DEPEND ON THE HOLY SPIRIT

"I, the Lord, search the heart, I try the mind, even to give every man according to his ways, and according to the fruit of his doings" (Jeremiah 17:10).

We can see in this verse four pointers that would help us to be led by the Holy Spirit.
1. *Let Him search your mind through His Word.*
2. *Stay firm in the midst of trials.*
3. *Remain in the right path without deviating.*
4. *Permanently bear fruit in the ministry allotted to us.*

CONCLUSION

If we want complete success in everything we do, we should depend totally on the Holy Spirit. As the Lord told us through the prophet Zechariah: *"Not by might, nor by power, but by My Spirit, says the Lord of hosts" (Zechariah 4:6).*

APPLICATION

Let there be a complete surrender of our lives to the Holy Spirit, renouncing any blockages - whether fears, insecurities, complexes, traumas or sins. Let the Holy Spirit fill every area of our lives.

THE ENCOUNTER PROGRAMME

In order to make the most of the weekend, the Encounter starts on Friday evening with a short meditation on the Word. A video or a short play showing God's original plan for mankind can be used so that the new believer will face the reality of his spiritual condition. After this there will be a time of reflection with the first lecture taking place the following morning.

SATURDAY

Lectures are in the following order:

1. *God's Fatherly Love: God is My Father*
2. *I Have Sinned Against the Lord*
3. *Seeing God Face to Face*
4. *Seeing What Jesus has Done for You on the Cross*
5. *Seeing What Your Sin did to Jesus*
6. *Ministry of the Cross*

Suggestion: On Saturday evening you can build a bonfire with the sin lists - all the sins people want to get rid of are burnt. This is a faith action that symbolises the total destruction of everything from the past, and the making of a firm commitment to live a life completely surrendered to Jesus Christ.

SUNDAY

Lectures:

1. *Faith to Heal Our Souls*
2. *Immersed in His Spirit*
3. *Water Baptism*
4. *A Vision for Success*

CLOSING THE ENCOUNTER

A reception can be arranged in the church or somewhere convenient, so that the different families can welcome the Encounter delegates back. Some of them can give their testimonies. The reception is very important, as it can be a great motivator for the disciple to continue with the process.

Encounter Talk No. 1

GOD'S FATHERLY LOVE: GOD IS MY FATHER

"[Jesus] said, 'A certain man had two sons. And the younger of them said to his father, "Father, give me the portion of goods that falls to me." So he divided to them his livelihood. And not many days after the younger son gathered all together, and journeyed to a far country, and there wasted his possessions with prodigal living. But when he had spent all, there arose a severe famine in that land, and he began to be in want. Then he went and joined himself to a citizen of that country, and he sent him into his fields to feed swine. And he would fain have filled his stomach with the pods that the swine ate, and no one gave him anything. But when he came to himself, he said, "How many of my father's hired servants have bread enough and to spare, and I perish with hunger! I will arise and go to my father, and will say to him, 'Father, I have sinned against heaven, and before you, and am no longer worthy to be called your son. Make me as one of your hired servants.'" And he arose and came to his father. But when he was still a great way off, his father saw him and had compassion, and ran, and fell on his neck, and kissed him. And the son said to him, "Father, I have sinned against heaven and in your sight, and am no longer worthy to be called your son." But the father said to his servants, "Bring out the best robe and put it on him, and put a ring on his hand and sandals on his feet. And bring the fatted calf here and kill it, and let us eat and be merry; for this my son was dead and is alive again; he was lost and is found." And they began to be merry.'"
(Luke 15:11-24).

GOAL

To lead everyone to genuine repentance, knowing the love of the Father.

INTRODUCTION

In Luke 15, we find one of the most moving and complete pictures of repentance, the prodigal son. It is a parable about the relentlessness of sin in a man's life. It shows how the ray of light shone in a sinner's mind and made him reflect on his actions, so that he began to change. It also shows the unfailing love of the Father, patiently waiting for His children to return home.

THE SON'S DECISION

There are three important steps in the process of genuine repentance:

1. **Renewing the mind.** (v. 17) He makes the decision to leave the sorry situation in which he finds himself, and returns home for a second chance.
2. **Making the right decision.** (v. 18) *"I will arise and go to my father..."* Repentance is to acknowledge your condition and to decide to return to the correct path.
3. **Confessing sins.** (v. 18b) *"...and will say to him, "Father, I have sinned against heaven and before you."'* Confession should be the result of a broken heart brought about by the acknowledgement of one's sin.
   "I acknowledged my sin to You... and You forgave the iniquity of my sin" (Psalm 32:5).

THE FATHER'S ATTITUDE

1. **He saw the son from afar.** (v. 20). God always looks at us with merciful eyes no matter how far we have gone away from Him.
2. **He was moved with compassion.** (v. 20). The sinner has offended God by his actions and has caused the Lord to be angry with him *(Isaiah 1:18)*. It doesn't matter how big the sin is; if we turn to the Father, He will reach out to us with His mercy and forgiveness.

the ladder of success
a practical guide

3. **He came out to meet him.** (v. 20) *"his father... ran and fell on his neck and kissed him.".* From the moment we take the decision to repent, the Lord runs to meet with each one of us, opening His arms, full of love to give us protection and security.

4. **He put the best clothes on him.** (v. 22) Shabby clothes represent sin. Justice is represented by new clothing. New clothes symbolise a total change in the inner man.

5. **He put a ring on his finger.** This shows that God restored the authority that was lost. Jesus gave us authority over every opposing power.

6. **He put shoes on his feet.** The Father trusts the son with the greatest ministry - preaching the gospel. For the believer this means the privilege of walking in full relationship with the divine word, and the ability to share it with others. The Apostle Paul said that we should clothe our feet with the preaching of the gospel (*Ephesians 6:15*).

7. **He restored his joy.** (v. 23) *"... let us eat and be merry."* The Christian life should be full of joy and this is represented by dancing.

CONCLUSION

It is necessary for the new believer to understand that genuine repentance means feeling pain for having done what was wrong, and that our heavenly Father is faithful and just to forgive us no matter how big our faults. Real repentance allows the Holy Spirit to work a real change in our lives.

APPLICATION

Lead people to real repentance in prayer, asking the Holy Spirit to bring brokenness into their hearts, and cry out for a genuine restoration for each person.

Encounter Talk No. 2

I HAVE SINNED AGAINST THE LORD

"Blessed is he whose transgression is forgiven, whose sin is covered. Blessed is the man to whom the Lord does not impute iniquity, and in whose spirit there is no deceit. When I kept silent, my bones grew old through my groaning all the day long. For day and night Your hand was heavy upon me; my vitality is turned into the drought of summer. I acknowledged my sin to You, and my iniquity have I not hidden. I said, 'I will confess my transgressions to the Lord', and You forgave the iniquity of my sin. For this cause every one that is godly shall pray to You in a time when You may be found; surely in a flood of great waters they shall not come near him. You are my hiding place; You shall preserve me from trouble; You shall surround me with songs of deliverance. I will instruct you and teach you in the way you should go; I will guide you with My eye. Do not be like the horse or like the mule, which have no understanding, which must be harnessed with bit and bridle, else they will not come near you. Many sorrows shall be to the wicked; but he who trusts in the Lord, mercy shall surround him. Be glad in the Lord and rejoice, you righteous; and shout for joy, all you upright in heart." (Psalm 32:1-11).

GOAL

To confront the person with his sin, its causes and consequences. Lead him to write them down, to renounce them and to make a decision to start a new life in Christ.

INTRODUCTION

David was the King of Israel and had the power to get whatever he wanted. He was not able to cover up his sin though, even when he tried to do it in every possible way. It became so public that even today we speak about David's sin. Everything that man does in secret, God will sooner or later expose in public. David, a man after God's heart, was the youngest among his brothers, obedient to his parents in everything. God saw the purity of his heart and chose him to be His servant. He was courageous in God, and was able to face fierce animals as well as the most hardened enemies. He did not know fear because he learned to fear God.

CAUSES LEADING DAVID TO SIN

- He did not go to war at the time he should have done so *(2 Samuel 11:1)*.

- He saw a naked woman and lusted after her in his heart. The Lord Jesus said: *"But I say to you that whoever looks at a woman to lust for her has already committed adultery with her in his heart" (Matthew 5:28)*. He did not care that she was a married woman. He only cared about his own pleasure. He tried to cover up his sin, and it led him to kill Uriah the Hittite, the husband of Bathsheba.

CONSEQUENCES OF SIN

Knowing that curses will never come without a cause, the following is what David experienced:

2 Samuel 12:7-12

- ***Financial blessing stops.*** *(v. 8)*
- ***The doors are opened to a spirit of violence.*** (v. 10)

- *It brings a curse.* (v. 11) *"I will raise up adversity against you..."*
- *We are exposed to public shame.* (v. 11-12) *"I will take your wives before your eyes and give them to your neighbour, and he shall lie with your wives in the sight of this sun."*
- *A spirit of infirmity and death comes upon the family.* (v. 14-15)

DAVID'S REPENTANCE

David was not conscious of the sin he had committed until Nathan the prophet confronted him. This brought such a conviction of sin that his repentance was genuine and he wrote about it in *Psalm 51.* Here he expressed his deep pain for offending God. He confessed his sin, renounced it, and pleaded for divine mercy.

DAVID'S LATER THOUGHTS

Years later David composed *Psalm 32,* where he expresses the joy of experiencing and obtaining divine forgiveness. He remembers three areas of his life that were affected:

The physical area. "My bones grew old". Satan looks for an argument to enter and take possession of a body through sickness *(Psalm 32:3-4).*

The emotional area. "...through my groaning all day long. For day and night your hand was heavy upon me". The person does not find any peace and constantly groans in his spirit *(Psalm 32:3).*

The financial area. "...my vitality was turned into the drought of summer". Dryness represents financial ruin *(Psalm 32:4).*

David remembers that because he confessed his sins he was forgiven and sanctified *(Psalm 32:5),* and from that moment forward he had the certainty that no trial or adversity would touch him *(Psalm 32:6).* There was a new song in his mouth, a song of deliverance *(Psalm 32:7).*

the ladder of success
a practical guide

CONCLUSION

When there is a genuine repentance, God completely wipes away all the sins that the person has committed. He separates them from us as far as the east is from the west and remembers them no more.

APPLICATION

We should lead every person to face his own sin. He should not hide, but confess and renounce them, and make a covenant to live a life of holiness from that day onward.

Encounter Talk No. 3.

SEEING GOD FACE TO FACE

*"So Jacob called the name of the place Peniel:
'For I have seen God face to face, and my life
was preserved.'" (Genesis 32:30).*

INTRODUCTION

Jacob is the believer's prototype. Though he had
the promise of blessing, he tried to obtain the
blessing through his own effort. This resulted in
him leading a double life until he had an encounter
face to face with God. This experience broke him
and he then began to walk in the right way.

JACOB'S EXAMPLE

God loved him before he was born: *"Jacob I loved
and Esau I hated."* Even from birth, he took hold of
his brother's heel to try to be born before him.
Cunningly he acquired the birthright from his brother and cleverly he disguised himself as Esau to
obtain the blessing. God protected Jacob. Even
when he was a liar and a cunning opportunist, God
was with him. Jacob took the decision to make a
covenant with God and committed himself to be a
faithful tither *(Genesis 28:20-22).* But what he sowed
he reaped. His father-in-law Laban deceived him
several times and he had to run away from his
father-in-law's house. Esau was planning to hurt
him but God spoke through dreams saying Jacob
should not be treated badly because he was His
servant.

JACOB'S BROKENNESS

When Jacob heard the news that his brother was going to meet him with four hundred armed men, fear gripped him. He remembered the earlier death threats that his brother had made against him.

This led him into intense and agonising prayer. God revealed Himself through an angel and Jacob wrestled with him all night long. *"And He said, 'Let me go, for the day breaks' but [Jacob] said, 'I will not let You go unless You bless me!'"* (Genesis 32:26). His perseverance in prayer led to a face-to-face encounter with God. It was then that deliverance for his soul took place. The next day, when he met his brother Esau, he said to him, *"...I have seen your face as though I had seen the face of God, and you were pleased with me"* (Genesis 33:10).

CONCLUSION

If we persevere in seeking God the way Jacob did, God will reveal Himself to us, and that encounter with Him will produce genuine deliverance in our hearts.

APPLICATION

Each person should seek the Lord in prayer until he has a face-to-face encounter with God.

Encounter Talk No. 4

SEEING WHAT JESUS HAS DONE FOR YOU ON THE CROSS

"...having wiped out the handwriting of requirements that was against us, which was contrary to us. And He has taken it out of the way, having nailed it to the cross. Having disarmed principalities and powers, He made a public spectacle of them, triumphing over them in it" (Colossians 2:14-15).

GOALS

For the believer to experience the three areas in which Jesus has redeemed us through the cross of Calvary.

INTRODUCTORY QUESTION

What are the steps to real repentance?
Jeremiah 33:3 says: "Call to me, and I will answer you, and show you great and mighty things, which you do not know."

REDEMPTION

Greek terms and meanings:
Agorazo - To buy in the marketplace (slaves).
Exagorazo - To buy and remove from the market-place (to make them no longer available for sale).
Lutroo - To loose (to free through paying a price). These are the three things Jesus did on the cross of Calvary. He gave His life - paying the highest price by shedding His blood. He bought us out of the slavery of sin and released us into total freedom. We were slaves to sin and under its control.

God became man and took the accusations that our adversary raised against us and cancelled them on the cross of Calvary. His blood was the price He paid for our redemption. Redemption covers the following areas of our lives.

AREAS OF REDEMPTION

- **Spiritual Area.** Redemption is the only door that leads man to an intimate relationship with the Author of Life. "Christ has redeemed us from the curse of the law, having become a curse for us (for it is written, 'Cursed is everyone who hangs on a tree')" (Galatians 3:13).

- **Physical Area.** Jesus delivers us from sickness which is a consequence of sin. *"Who Himself bore our sins in His own body on the tree, that we, having died to sins, might live for righteousness - by whose stripes you were healed" (1 Peter 2:24).*

- **Financial Area.** Jesus delivers us from poverty, misery and all financial curses. *"For you know the grace of our Lord Jesus Christ, that though He was rich, yet for your sakes He became poor, that you through His poverty might become rich" (2 Corinthians 8:9).*

The cross: The only way for the cancellation of debt. The first Adam failed and brought the curse. Jesus, the second Adam, had to live in holiness and bear the consequences of sin, receiving upon His body all the punishment that mankind deserved. At Gethsemane, Jesus agonised in prayer when He saw everything that was coming His way; His mission was centred on the cross of Calvary.

THE POWER OF THE CROSS

"For the message of the cross is foolishness to those who are perishing, but to us who are being saved it is the power of God" (1 Corinthians 1:18).

The message of the cross is that of humility: Jesus being God became man and died for us. It is a message of peace. Jesus came to unite people's hearts, to make one people out of two, taking away the walls that separated the Jews and Gentiles, slaves and free people, men and women, and uniting them as one. The message of the cross set us free from demonic bondage, fear, trauma and oppression. It is a word of love: *"For God so loved the world that He gave His only begotten Son, that whoever believes in Him should not perish but have everlasting life" (John 3:16).*

Among other things, Jesus:

- became Son of Man that I may become son of God *(John 1:12)*.
- became sin that I may become the righteousness of God *(2 Corinthians 5:21)*.
- became a curse so that I may enjoy His blessings *(Galatians 3:13)*.
- became sick so that I may be healed *(Isaiah 53:4-5)*.
- became poor so that through His poverty I may become rich *(2 Corinthians 8:9)*.
- died my death so that I may live His life *(Galatians 2:20, 1 John 5:11-13)*.
- was defeated on the cross so that I may be victorious *(Romans 8:37)*.
- came to earth through natural birth, so that we may enter into the kingdom of God through spiritual birth.

the ladder of success a practical guide

- came to live in our home, the earth, so that we could live in His home, heaven.
- clothed Himself as man so that we can be clothed with the Spirit of God.

FINAL QUESTION

What did the cross do in your life?

APPLICATION

We can permanently enjoy the victory of the cross in three areas: spiritual, physical and financial!

Encounter Talk No. 5

FAITH TO HEAL OUR SOULS

"A merry heart makes a cheerful countenance, but by sorrow of the heart the spirit is broken" (Proverbs 15:13).

GOALS

To bring healing of the soul and emotions to the new believer. To confront the new believer with problems in relationships, so that he will live in peace and acceptance.

INTRODUCTORY QUESTIONS

What is it that most commonly hurts people?
In whom were we accepted since the beginning of time before we experienced any type of rejection? *(Ephesians 1:4)*

INTRODUCTION

Man was created by God to live with others. Man needs acceptance, love and security. There is no question that rejection is one of the most painful feelings. Rejection weakens the will until it is broken. Therefore it is necessary to identify at each stage of one's life how rejection occurred and begin to heal the wounds. Some areas of rejection:

1. IN THE MOTHER'S WOMB

"For He chose us in Him before the foundation of the world, that we should be holy and without blame before Him..." (Ephesians 1:4). We were chosen by God before the foundation of the world, He formed us in our mother's womb: *"Your hands have made me and fashioned me..." (Job 10:8).* And David said: *"Your eyes saw my substance, being yet unformed. And in Your book they all were written, the days fashioned for me, when as yet there were none of them" (Psalm 139:16).*

Encounter Talk No. 6

IMMERSED IN HIS SPIRIT

"I indeed baptise you with water unto repentance, but He who is coming after me is mightier than I, whose sandals I am not worthy to carry. He will baptise you with the Holy Spirit and with fire" (Matthew 3:11).

Verse to memorise

"But you shall receive power when the Holy Spirit has come upon you; and you shall be witnesses to Me in Jerusalem, and in all Judea and Samaria, and to the end of the earth" (Acts 1:8).

GOALS

For the person to receive the baptism of the Holy Spirit with the evidence of speaking in other tongues.

INTRODUCTORY QUESTIONS

Do you give good gifts to your children?
"If you then, being evil, know how to give good gifts to your children, how much more will your heavenly Father give the Holy Spirit to those who ask Him?" (Luke 11:13).

INTRODUCTION

We can be immersed in the Spirit of God through the baptism of the Holy Spirit.
It is a unique experience. It is the Spirit who joins us to the body of Christ, who governs and leads us. He gives us the mind of Christ, controls our tongue and produces a total transformation in our lives. His presence flows like rivers of living water inside our being. If we want to have successful lives, we need the Holy Spirit, the Breath of Life, who teaches us.

SEALED AS SONS OF GOD

"In Him you also trusted, after you heard the word of truth, the gospel of your salvation; in whom also, having believed, you were sealed with the Holy Spirit of promise, who is the guarantee of our inheritance until the redemption of the purchased possession, to the praise of His glory" (Ephesians 1:13-14).

Receiving the Holy Spirit brings us the guarantee that we are children of God. The Holy Spirit is the best gift God can give us, as Doctor Luke expresses it in Luke 11:11-13. In order to receive the fullness of the Holy Spirit we must not allow our bodies to sin. Romans 6:13 says, *"And do not present your members as instruments of unrighteousness to sin, but present yourselves to God as being alive from the dead, and your members as instruments of righteousness to God."*

THE HOLY SPIRIT IS RECEIVED BY FREE WILL

The Holy Spirit is the entrance to a life full of rich experiences. One of them is genuine freedom. *"Now the Lord is the Spirit; and where the Spirit of the Lord is, there is liberty" (2 Corinthians 3:17).* We received the Holy Spirit the moment we believed in Jesus. Paul told the people at Ephesus: *"'Did you receive the Holy Spirit when you believed?' So they said to him, 'We have not so much as heard whether there is a Holy Spirit.' And he said unto them, 'Into what then were you baptised?' So they said, 'Into John's baptism.' Then Paul said, 'John indeed baptised with a baptism of repentance, saying to the people that they should believe on Him who would come after him, that is, on Christ Jesus.' When they heard this, they were baptised in the name of the Lord Jesus. And when Paul had laid his hands on them, the Holy Spirit came upon them, and they spoke with tongues and prophesied." (Acts 19:2-6)*

the ladder of success

a practical guide

The baptism of the Holy Spirit empowers us.
"But you shall receive power when the Holy Spirit has come upon you; and you shall be witnesses to Me in Jerusalem, and in all Judea and Samaria, and to the end of the earth" (Acts 1:8).

WHO IS THE HOLY SPIRIT?

1. **In the Greek He is called the Helper.** The Greek word '*parakletos*' means somebody who is called beside us to help.

2. **He is a person.** He has all the attributes of a person, like the Father and the Son.
   1 Corinthians 2:11 says, "For what man knows the things of a man, except the spirit of man which is in him? Even so no one knows the things of God except the Spirit of God."

3. **The One who anoints.** The presence of the Holy Spirit in our lives equates to having the anointing of God flowing through us.
   "How God anointed Jesus of Nazareth with the Holy Spirit and with power, who went about doing good and healing all who were oppressed by the Devil, for God was with him" (Acts 10:38).

4. **We can be conscious of His presence.**
   "'He who believes in Me, as the scripture has said, out of his heart will flow rivers of living water.' But this He spoke concerning the Spirit, whom those believing in Him would receive; for the Holy Spirit was not yet given; because Jesus was not yet glorified" (John 7:38-39).

5. **He causes us to be born again.** Jesus said:
   "Most assuredly, I say to you, unless one is born of water and the Spirit, he cannot enter into the kingdom of God. That which is born of the flesh is flesh, and that which is born of the Spirit is spirit" (John 3:5-6).

6. **He leads us into all truth.** *"However, when He, the Spirit of truth, has come, He will guide you into all truth; for He will not speak on His own authority, but whatever He hears He will speak; and He will tell you things to come" (John 16:13).*

7. **He reveals divine secrets.** *"Furthermore, when I came to Troas to preach Christ's gospel, a door was opened to me by the Lord" (2 Corinthians 2:12).*

FINAL QUESTION

Are you ready to allow the power of the Holy Spirit to come into your life?

APPLICATION

There are three fundamental steps to receive the fullness of the Holy Spirit with the evidence of speaking in tongues.

- *Be sure that your life has been completely sanctified with the blood of Christ.*

- *Wholeheartedly ask the Son to baptise you with His Holy Spirit with the evidence of speaking in tongues.*

- *Persevere in prayer believing. Do not be discouraged. Persevere until you have received the fullness of the Spirit flowing through your life.*

the ladder of success
a practical guide

WATER BAPTISM

"In Him you were also circumcised with the circumcision made without hands, by putting off the body of the sins of the flesh, by the circumcision of Christ, buried with Him in baptism, in which you also were raised with Him through faith in the working of God, who raised Him from the dead"
(Colossians 2:11-12).

VERSE TO MEMORISE

"You have heard Him and have been taught by Him, as the truth is in Jesus: that you put off, concerning your former conduct, the old man which grows corrupt according to the deceitful lusts"
(Ephesians 4:21-22).

Related text: Matthew 28:19.

GOALS

For the person to experience what Jesus experienced when the heavens opened and the voice of God was heard saying: *"this is my beloved Son with whom I am well pleased."* Then He was filled with the Holy Spirit.

INTRODUCTORY QUESTIONS

What is the main prerequisite to being baptised? *(Mark 16:16)*
Why be baptised? *(1 John 2:6)*

WHY BE BAPTISED?

To fulfil all righteousness.
"But Jesus answered and said to him, 'Permit it to be so now, for thus it is fitting for us to fulfil all righteousness.' Then he allowed Him" (Matthew 3:15).
To follow the example Jesus set for us. Christ set the model in everything so that we should follow in His footsteps *(1 Peter 2:21).*

To set us free from the curse of sin. *(Acts 2:37-38)*
It symbolises burial. *(Colossians 2:12)*
It clothes us in Christ. *(Galatians 3:27)*

PREREQUISITES TO BEING BAPTISED

- Receive Christ as Lord and Saviour. *(John 1:12)*
- Have faith to take the next step after being saved. *(Mark 16:15)*
- Show evidence of true repentance. *(Luke 3:7-8)*
- Have a generous heart. *(Luke 3:11)*
- Be upright in all your dealings. *(Luke 3:13)*
- Be glad with what God has given you. *(Luke 3:14)*

BENEFITS OF BAPTISM

- Jesus' death becomes our death, and His resurrection our new birth. *(Romans 6:3-4)*
- We are planted and can grow. *(Romans 6:5-6)*
- We can come before God as those that are living among the dead. *(Romans 6:13)*
- Sin cannot rule over us. *(Romans 6:14)*
- We are servants of righteousness. *(Romans 6:18)*
- We are servants of God. We are sanctified and have eternal life. *(Romans 6:22)*

WHO CAN BE BAPTISED?

Everyone who believes. *(Mark 16:16)*

WHO BAPTISES?

The pastor or an authorised leader.

PURPOSE OF BAPTISM

To be identified with Christ in obedience.
To join the body of Christ.

the ladder of success
a practical guide

RESULT OF BAPTISM

The power of Christ is upon you and works
through your life.

FINAL QUESTION

Did you experience the new birth after you were
baptised? Or did you get baptised after
being born again?

APPLICATION

Water baptism symbolises death to the old nature,
burial and resurrection to a new life. It enables you
to leave behind the old way of living and open your
life for God to fulfil His purposes.

Encounter Talk No. 8

A VISION OF SUCCESS

"Now the LORD said to Abram: 'Get out of your country, from your family and from your father's house, to a land that I will show you. I will make you a great nation; I will bless you and make your name great; and you shall be a blessing'" (Genesis 12:1-2).

Verse to memorise
"Therefore go and make disciples of all nations, baptising them in the name of the Father and of the Son and of the Holy Spirit" (Matthew 28:19).

GOALS

To understand that the vision has been birthed in the heart of God and to know it will allow us to advance and to become successful leaders.

INTRODUCTORY QUESTION

What are the blessings that God has for us?
(3 John 2)

FOUR ASPECTS OF THE BLESSING

- *I will make of you a great nation*
- *I will bless you*
- *I will make your name great*
- *You will be a blessing*

AREAS INCLUDED IN THE BLESSING

- *Physical*
- *Emotional*
- *Spiritual*
- *Family*
- *Professional*
- *Social*

the ladder of success
a practical guide

PREPARING TO RECEIVE THE BLESSING

There are four steps to achieving success:

1. **Win** *(Matthew 28:18-20)*
2. **Consolidate** *(The care we should give to new believers)*
3. **Disciple** *(Luke 14:25-33)*
4. **Send** *(Matthew 28:19)*

FINAL QUESTION

What is your next step within the vision when you return from the Encounter?

APPLICATION

You have already taken the first steps in your spiritual development. Continue to develop commitment within the vision. Become an active disciple, be part of a cell, and stay close to your leader, who will guide you.

POST-ENCOUNTER

Venue:	In the church or hall.
Teacher:	Preferably a pastor.
Duration:	An hour a week for three months.

GOAL

To show the disciple, just back from the Encounter, how to deal with the attacks of Satan. It will also teach the disciple how to relate to the world, friends and problems and how to overcome temptation, the flesh, sin, the world and the Devil.

Many people lose their way after the Encounter. Satan prepares a counter-attack after having lost ground in their lives. The newly encountered person needs to be equipped to resist these attacks. The introduction of the four-week Post-Encounter teaching produced greater fruit. People who go on Encounters are also given an extended three-month period of spiritual assistance. This has resulted in an unprecedented increase in the retention of new believers.

CONTENTS

- *How to face the world*
- *What is the world?*
- *How does the world affect me?*
- *How do I confront the world now that I am a Christian?*

the ladder of success
a practical guide

How to speak with God

- The importance of prayer.
- How can you have an effective prayer time?

Social Life

- Our first challenge: The people around us.
- How do we behave before non-believers?
- Taking on the challenge of winning your friends.

The Word: Fountain of Life

- How can I get closer to the Word?
- How can I study the Word?
- Benefits of getting closer to the Word.

Sexuality

- Sex as something created by God.
- Why wait and not have sexual relations outside marriage?
- How to avoid sinful sexual relations?

The Church: God's Refuge

- What is the Church?
- Why do we need the Church?

A Balanced Life

- The intellectual aspect.
- The physical aspect.
- The spiritual aspect.
- The social aspect.

Baptism, a Step of Obedience

- What is baptism?
- Types of water baptism.
- Prerequisites to being baptised.
- The blessing of baptism.

Music and its Influence in our Lives

- The plan of the enemy through music.
- What Satan wants to achieve through music.
- Christian music - gives life.
- How to fight against demonic music now that I am a Christian?

How do I get to know the Will of God?

- Benefits of obeying the will of God.
- How can I know the will of God?

disciple

DISCIPLE

GOAL

To prepare efficient cell leaders with the ability to win lives for Christ, who can continue to disciple new believers until they become successful leaders.

WHAT IS DISCIPLESHIP?

It is a programme of simple teaching, orientated to practical things, which motivates the students to learn themselves. This training takes place in the classroom. The student gains practical experience through the cells. The discipleship programme is specifically designed for new believers.

WHO IS IT FOR?

It is for those who have completed an Encounter and attended the Post-Encounter teachings. The lectures are the same for all of the nets.

DURATION

Three terms and three months to write the thesis.

TIMETABLE

Once a week, two hours per class, one hour per subject.

SUBJECTS (TOPICS)

One hour each for the lectures and the seminars taken from a range of topics.

SCHOOL OF LEADERS PROGRAM

FIRST TERM LEVEL 1

LECTURE		SEMINAR 1			
		MEN'S NET	WOMEN'S NET	COUPLES' NET	YOUTH NET
1.	Salvation	Men's sexuality	Purpose of life	God's prosperity for couples	Family I
2.	The old man and old nature	Principles for a successful Christian family I	God values women	Learning to deal with irritation among couples	Family II
3.	Repentance	Principles for a successful Christian family II	Developing your character	Three cornerstones to build the house on	Family III
4.	The Bible	You can be prosperous	Grow to your fullness	The advantage of being two	Family IV
5.	Prayer	The leader's character	Thank God for being a woman	Building a family	Courting I
6.	Water baptism	Integrity as a lifestyle	The family is in God's heart	Give your children to the Lord	Courting II
7.	Faith	Finding the right friends	The woman's role in the Bible	Loving obedience	Courting III
8.	The Holy Spirit	Integrity	Developing relationships in the family	Prayer to change families	Courting IV
9.	Laying on of hands	How to pray and get an answer	Principles for a happy family	The family needs the Holy Spirit	Abundant life I
10.	How to overcome obstacles		Prepare for excellence	The family's priesthood	Abundant life II

Second Level - Lectures

1. *Cells for growth*
2. *The vision*
3. *Personal preparation to lead a cell*
4. *The structure of a cell*
5. *Methodology of a cell*
6. *Strategies for success*
7. *Motivation for growth*
8. *How to solve problems in the cell*
9. *Guidelines for choosing a leadership team*
10. *Relationship between the leader and the disciples*

Second Level - Seminars

- *Intercession (4 sessions)*
- *Evangelism (4 sessions)*
- *Service (2 sessions)*

Third Level - Lectures

1. *What does it mean to be a leader?*
2. *The calling*
3. *The leader's personality (2 sessions)*
4. *The cost of leadership*
5. *Principles for excellence in leadership*
6. *Dangers of leadership*
7. *Types of leadership*
8. *Practical advice for preaching (2 sessions)*

Third Level - Seminars

- *Consolidation (2 sessions)*
- *Holy Spirit (3 sessions)*
- *Counselling (5 sessions)*

THESIS

After attending the School of Leaders the disciple should present a thesis on a simple and practical topic. Working under the supervision of a teacher, this will take between three and six months to prepare. By this time they should have considerably developed their cell and be well on the way to forming their twelve.

SCHOOL OF TEACHERS

All the experience gained in the School of Leaders will prepare leaders to form their twelve. Having formed their twelve and then their 144 the disciples should start planning the organising of their own Encounters and School of Leaders. They will therefore need to learn how to teach others. This will be another stage of their training. Hence, there is continuous training, as leaders must strive for excellence in all that they do.

the ladder of success
a practical guide

THE RE-ENCOUNTER

WHEN TO DO IT?

During the second level of the School of Leaders.

WHAT IS IT?

The Re-Encounter is a new Encounter where the disciple in training receives more in-depth ministry. This will prepare them to minister through the cells.

WHO IS IT FOR?

Those who have finished the first level of the School of Leaders.

DURATION

A long weekend, it could be three or four days.

SUGGESTED TOPICS

1. The responsibility of the Christian in the world
2. What is Christ doing in me?
3. The traumas of family life
4. Emotional traumas
5. Your image and self-esteem
6. Temperament
7. What Christ has done for me
8. The spiritual realm
9. The armour of God
10. Identifying bondages and curses
11. Conquering each area with spiritual warfare
12. What Christ can do through me
13. Consecration
14. The leader and ethics
15. Ethics - behaviour
16. The fruit and gifts of the Spirit

WEEKEND LECTURES

Some subjects can take more time than is normally allocated to classes. These could be covered over a weekend, a Friday night, a Saturday or at a more convenient time.
These subjects are: Evangelism, Consolidation and Encounter.

THE ENCOUNTER MATERIAL

What do we mean by Encounter?
The Encounter material can be taught in six hours.

GOAL

To provide the cell leader with a solid biblical basis and reference material for his discipling work.

Subjects

- *The new birth*
- *Advantages of the new birth*
- *How to attain the new birth*
- *Spiritual babies*
- *Water baptism*
- *Making prayer a way of life*
- *Knowing the power of the Scriptures*
- *Knowing the Holy Spirit*
- *God is seeking us*
- *The divine purpose for man*
- *Bridges leading nowhere*
- *Jesus Christ: the only true bridge*
- *The power of the cross*
- *The cross sets us free from sin*
- *The cross sets us free*

- *The cross breaks all curses*
- *The cross heals all afflictions*
- *The seven words of victory*

CONSOLIDATION

WHAT IS IT?
Training for the consolidators who will work together with the new disciple from the moment of commitment until the home visit.

MATERIAL	*Consolidation: An Effective Process for Making Disciples by Claudia Fajardo*
DURATION	*Six hours*

After the seminar the disciple reads the book and works through the exercises in each chapter.

GOAL

To train the consolidation teams on how to act at each stage of consolidation. When the altar call is made in the church, making the 'telephone visit', visiting the new disciple at home, and placing them in a cell group.

Subjects
- *Consolidation - an effective process for making disciples*
- *Principles of consolidation*
- *Getting ready to consolidate*
- *Prayer that overcomes*
- *Salvation*
- *Five teachings on evangelism*
- *Verifying salvation*
- *Allocation*
- *The 'telephone visit'*

- *The home visit*
- *Short sermons:*
  - Fear
  - Spiritual growth
  - Family problems
  - Depression
  - Guidance
  - Finances
  - Health
  - How to overcome temptation
  - Rejection
  - Courtship
  - Objections

THE IMPORTANCE OF EVANGELISM

Bible Verse:

"And Jesus came and spoke to them, saying, 'All authority has been given to Me in heaven and on earth. Go therefore and make disciples of all the nations, baptising them in the name of the Father and of the Son and of the Holy Spirit, teaching them to observe all things that I have commanded you; and lo, I am with you always, even to the end of the age.' Amen." (Matthew 28:18-20).

SIX FUNDAMENTAL PRINCIPLES FOR EVANGELISM

A. It is a command from the Lord
Before giving the Great Commission, Jesus told His disciples: "Remember, I have all authority in the universe. With the assurance that I have overcome, go and do the work because I will be with you".

B. Jesus is the model for evangelism
Luke 6:17-19: "And He came down with them and stood on a level place with a crowd of His disciples and a great multitude of people from all Judea and Jerusalem, and from the seacoast of Tyre and Sidon, who came to hear Him and be healed of their diseases,

the ladder of success a practical guide

as well as those who were tormented with unclean spirits. And they were healed. And the whole multitude sought to touch Him, for power went out from Him and healed them all."

We can see five principles exhibited by Jesus:
1. He shared the gospel with the multitudes without looking at where they came from
2. He captured the attention of the people and they listened to Him attentively
3. He healed the sick
4. He set free all the demon-possessed
5. He was permanently flowing in the power of the Holy Spirit

The Apostle Peter wrote in 1Peter 2:21, *"For to this you were called, because Christ also suffered for us, leaving us an example, that you should follow His steps."*

C. Soul winning has to be the heartbeat of our lives

"But when He saw the multitudes, He was moved with compassion for them, because they were weary and scattered, like sheep having no shepherd. Then He said to His disciples, 'The harvest truly is plentiful, but the labourers are few. Therefore pray the Lord of the harvest to send out labourers into His harvest'" (Matthew 9:36-38).

We can see two areas where the Lord wants to minister:

● *Compassion for the lost*
● *Life of prayer*

The Apostle Paul, in his letter to the Galatians, says: *"My little children, for whom I labour in birth again until Christ is formed in you"* (Galatians 4:19). And to the Corinthians he says, *"For if I preach the gospel, I have nothing to boast of, for necessity is laid upon me; yes, woe is me if I do not preach the gospel!"* (1 Corinthians 9:16). Then he adds, *"to the weak*

I became as weak, that I might win the weak. I have become all things to all men, that I might by all means save some. Now this I do for the gospel's sake, that I may be partaker of it with you" (1 Corinthians. 9:22-23).

During Paul's final speech at Miletus, he told Ephesian elders: *"But none of these things move me; nor do I count my life dear to myself, so that I may finish my race with joy, and the ministry which I received from the Lord Jesus, to testify to the gospel of the grace of God"* (Acts 20:24).

D. Work under the leading of the Holy Spirit

"Nevertheless I tell you the truth. It is to your advantage that I go away; for if I do not go away, the Helper will not come to you; but if I depart, I will send Him to you. And when He has come, He will convict the world of sin, and of righteousness, and of judgement: of sin, because they do not believe in Me; of righteousness, because I go to My Father and you see Me no more; of judgement, because the ruler of this world is judged" (John 16:7-11).

We can see three fundamental ways in which the Holy Spirit works in the life of each individual:

He convicts of sin. Nobody can truly repent if the Holy Spirit does not show them the magnitude of their sin.

He convicts of righteousness. This is the righteousness that God gave us through His Son Jesus Christ. His redeeming work on the cross of Calvary cancelled all the arguments that were against us.

He convicts of judgement. The same God who judged the adversary at the cross of Calvary will, one day, judge all mankind before His throne. The early church recognised the Holy Spirit as an important member of the leadership team. He was the one who took the decisions: *"For it seemed good to the Holy Spirit, and to us, to lay upon you no greater burden than these necessary things: that you abstain from things offered to idols, from blood, from things strangled, and from sexual immorality. If you keep yourselves from these, you will do well"* (Acts 15:28-29).

E. Different ways to evangelise

Personal evangelism

Jesus had direct contact with many individuals.
Through these relationships He was able to present the gospel in a clear way. He told Nicodemus
that he had to be born again *(John 3).* He introduced Himself as the fountain of living waters to
the Samaritan woman *(John 4).* He told the leper:
"*...I am willing, be clean*", and He told the centurion:
"*... go, as you believe it will be done*" *(Matthew 8).*

Jesus visited homes

At the home of Simon the Pharisee, Jesus taught a
great principle: *He who has been forgiven much,
loves much; he who is forgiven little, loves little
(see Luke 7).* At the home of Simon Peter, Jesus
healed his mother-in-law of a fever. Then He set
free many who were oppressed by demons and
healed the sick. He visited Jairus' home and
brought his dead daughter back to life *(Matthew 9).*
Jesus often visited Martha and Mary's home. And
when He heard about the death of Lazarus Jesus
went to resurrect him.

Jesus and the multitudes

Thousands received the Word of God when He
preached the Sermon on the Mount *(Matthew 5).*

John 6 speaks about the multitudes that followed
Jesus. He had compassion on them, made them
sit down and fed them with only five loaves and two
fishes *(John 6:1-14).* On another occasion the disciples said to him: "*You see the multitude thronging
You, and You say, 'Who touched Me?*'" *(Mark 5:31).*

F. Effective evangelism

● Appropriate preparation. *"Be diligent to present yourself approved to God, a worker who does not need to be ashamed, rightly dividing the word of truth" (2 Timothy 2:15).*

● Confess Jesus Christ publicly. *"...whoever confesses Me before men, him I will also confess before My Father who is in heaven" (Matthew 10:32).*

● Live anointed life. *"Salt is good; but if the salt has lost its flavour, how shall it be seasoned? It is neither fit for the land nor for the dunghill, but men throw it out. He who has ears to hear, let him hear!" (Luke 14:34-35).*

● Have faith to break down obstacles. *"So the Lord said, 'If you have faith as a mustard seed, you can say to this mulberry tree, Be pulled up by the roots and be planted in the sea, and it would obey you'" (Luke 17:6).*

● Be diligent in sharing the gospel. *"And when Jesus came to the place, He looked up and saw him, and said to him, 'Zaccheus, make haste and come down, for today I must stay at your house.'" (Luke 19:5) "Do you not say, 'There are still four months and then comes the harvest'? Behold, I say to you, lift up your eyes and look at the fields, for they are already white for harvest!" (John 4:35).*

send

SEND

. . . A DIVINE COMMAND

The prophet Isaiah saw one of the greatest divine revelations. He saw the Lord seated on His throne of glory and saw the seraphim that continually worship Him saying, *"Holy, Holy, Holy"*. Then he heard the Lord who said to him, *"Whom shall I send, who will go for us?"* The prophet's response was, *"Here am I, send me" (Isaiah 6:8).*

Afterwards the prophet confirmed his calling by the Lord when he said, *"...the Lord God and His Spirit have sent me" (Isaiah 48:16).*

The prophet Jeremiah was called in a similar way when the Lord said to him, *"Before I formed you in the womb I knew you; Before you were born I sanctified you; I ordained you a prophet to the nations." Then said I: "Ah, Lord GOD! Behold, I cannot speak, for I am a youth." But the LORD* said to me: *"Do not say, 'I am a youth,' For you shall go to all to whom I send you, And whatever I command you, you shall speak" (Jeremiah 1:5-7).* The prophet fell into deep depression afterwards, saying, *"'I will not make mention of Him, nor speak anymore in His name.' But His word was in my heart like a burning fire shut up in my bones; I was weary of holding it back, and I could not" (Jeremiah 20:9).*

Though the early prophets made every effort to please the Lord, this was not enough. God was asking for greater effort and sacrifice. The only one able to fulfil the requirements was His Son Jesus Christ. That is why a prophecy was given in the book of Psalms: *"Sacrifice and offering You did not desire; my ears You have opened. Burnt offering and sin offering You did not require. Then I said, 'Behold, I come; In the scroll of the book it is written of me. I delight to do Your will, O my God, and Your law is within my heart'" (Psalms 40:6-8).*

the ladder of success
a practical guide

This confirms what the writer of the book of Hebrews says. *"For it is not possible that the blood of bulls and goats could take away sins. Therefore, when He came into the world, He said 'Sacrifice and offering You did not desire, But a body You have prepared for Me. In burnt offerings and sacrifices for sin You had no pleasure.' Then I said, 'Behold, I have come... In the volume of the book it is written of Me... to do Your will, O, God'"* (Hebrews 10:4-7).

In the sermon that Jesus preached concerning the bread of life, He said, *"Do not labour for the food which perishes, but for the food which endures to everlasting life, which the Son of Man will give you, because God the Father has set His seal on Him"* (John 6:27).

In the book of Revelation, the Apostle John heard a great voice saying, *"'Who is worthy to open the scroll and to loose its seals?' And no one in heaven or on the earth or under the earth was able to open the scroll, or to look at it. So I wept much, because no one was found worthy to open and read the scroll, or to look at it. But one of the elders said to me, 'Do not weep. Behold, the Lion of the tribe of Judah, the Root of David, has prevailed to open the scroll and to loose its seven seals'"* (Revelation 5:2-5).

We can see some of the aspects of the call of Christ that John points out in the sixth chapter of his gospel:

- *The Father indicated it. "This is the work of God, that you believe in Him whom He sent." (v. 29)*
- *We should believe in Him. "For the bread of God is He who comes down from heaven and gives life to the world." (v. 33)*
- *He truly is the bread of life. "And Jesus said to them, 'I am the bread of life. He who comes to Me shall never hunger, and he who believes in Me shall never thirst." (v. 35)*
- *He did not come to do His own will, but the will of the One who sent Him. "For I have come down from heaven, not to do My own will, but the will of Him who sent Me." (v. 38)*
- *He came from God. "This is the will of the Father*

who sent Me, that of all He has given Me I should lose nothing, but should raise it up at the last day" *(v. 39).*
● *He saw the Father. "And this is the will of Him who sent Me, that everyone who sees the Son and believe in Him may have everlasting life; and I will raise him up at the last day" (v. 40).*
● *Whoever receives Him will live. "As the living Father sent Me, and I live because of the Father, so he who feeds on Me will live because of Me" (v. 57).*

After the Lord arose from the dead, He appeared to His disciples and told them, *"'Peace to you! As the Father has sent Me, I also send you.' And when He had said this, He breathed on them, and said to them, 'Receive the Holy Spirit'"* (John 20:21-22).

The Apostle Paul said, *"And how shall they preach unless they are sent? As it is written: 'How beautiful are the feet of those who preach the gospel of peace, Who bring glad tidings of good things!'"* (Romans 10:15).

GOING TO CONQUER

During the time of Moses the people of Israel left Egypt, reached the boundaries of Canaan and went to conquer the Promised Land. Moses chose twelve men and sent them to inspect the territory of Canaan. He sent them as spies, telling them to bring a full report about the land. They were told to:

● *Observe how the land was and bring a general description of the territory.*
● *Find out about the people who lived in it. Were they strong or weak? To find out what kind of people they would be facing.*
● *Discover how the territory was populated and to know what principalities were dominating the region.*
● *See if the land was good or bad and to know if it was to be a blessing or a curse.*
● *Find out how the cities were built. Were they just camps or fortified cities? This would help them know what sort of faith was going to be required.*

- *To see whether the soil was fertile or barren. This shows we should have clear understanding of the spiritual environment. We need to know if the people are ready to receive the gospel or there is a need for strong intercessory work first.*
- *Were there trees or not? This refers to whether the people were bearing fruit or not (Numbers 13:17-20).*

The directions given by Moses were appropriate. But Moses had not taken care first to train the twelve spies and they were lacking in character. They were shocked and frightened by what they saw. When they came with their report, its content was highly negative. The exceptions were Caleb and Joshua. They gave a report full of faith and optimism because they had a different spirit. The outcome was that Israel had to spend forty years in the wilderness in loneliness, shortage, sadness and affliction. God wanted to teach them that man does not live by bread alone but by every word that comes out of His mouth. All the time they had to spend in the wilderness was because character had not been formed in ten of the twelve spies.

ESTABLISHMENT OF THE GOVERNMENT OF TWELVE

After forty years, Joshua was commissioned by God to conquer the Promised Land. The Lord gave him specific instructions on what he should do to conquer it:

Joshua 1. The Lord prepared him to enter and conquer the promised land *(v. 3).* He told him that every place he set his feet would be his.
Joshua 2. He sent twelve spies to inspect the Promised Land. These are prototypes of the Holy Spirit and Jesus the Word of God.
Joshua 3. All the children of Israel crossed the Jordan. This symbolises water baptism.
Joshua 4. Establishment of the Government of Twelve. *"Take for yourselves twelve men from the people, one man from every tribe, and command them, saying, 'Take for yourselves twelve stones from*

here, out of the midst of the Jordan, from the place where the priests' feet stood firm. You shall carry them over with you and leave them in the lodging place where you lodge tonight'" (Joshua 4:2-3). During the night they had no light. This shows, therefore, that they had to get the stones by faith. This is a picture of how the Lord chose His twelve by faith during a night of prayer *(v. 5)*. Each one of the twelve had to choose a stone and carry it on his shoulders - indicating ministerial responsibility. These stones were to come from the midst of the Jordan, representing lives that have gone through a process of testing *(v. 7)*. God divided the Jordan so that the people could pass through on dry ground showing that the wilderness, with all its limitations and needs, was completely left behind *(v. 20)*. Joshua set up the twelve stones at Gilgal as a memorial to what the powerful hand of God is able to do and so that the people of Israel would fear Him continually *(v. 24)*. Also at Gilgal, Joshua circumcised the people of Israel for the second time *(Joshua 5:2)* symbolising the spiritual circumcision in the heart of a believer. Then there was a celebration of the Passover together, the establishment of the Communion and fellowship of one with another.

We can see that there were different stages in the life of the patriarch, Joshua. First, God gave him a vision concerning the conquest of Jericho. Then He gave him directions through the spies' report. After this he had to cross the Jordan, which symbolises baptism. Then came the circumcision and communion that symbolise the transformation in our spiritual lives and that the stain of sin has been removed so that we have communion with God and our neighbours.

the ladder of success a practical guide

In verses 13-15 of chapter 5, we read of the angel that came to Joshua to help him during the battle for Jericho. Using the strategy given to him, Joshua took the city (chapter 6). In chapter 7, God taught a great lesson about the importance of remaining in complete holiness in order to gain His victory. Chapter 8 shows Joshua, once again, receiving strategies for war from the Lord. Chapter 9 teaches about the dangers of entering into an alliance with unknown people. And in chapter 10 God shows His authority in the fight at Gibeon. Chapters 11 and 12 detail Joshua's possession of the land and evaluate the portion that had been occupied and what was still to conquer.

WHY THE TWELVE?

"But when He saw the multitudes, He was moved with compassion for them, because they were weary and scattered, like sheep having no shepherd. Then He said to His disciples, 'The harvest truly is plentiful, but the labourers are few. Therefore pray the Lord of the harvest to send out labourers into His harvest.' And when He had called His twelve disciples to Him, He gave them power over unclean spirits, to cast them out, and to heal all kinds of sickness and all kinds of disease" (Matthew 9:36-10:1).

The Lord saw the people and had compassion on them. That is why he chose twelve men to meet their needs. He gave them authority, then sent them out to expel demons and heal every sickness. Jesus invested most of His ministry in forming these twelve disciples. He had a very specific goal which was to reproduce His character in the lives of these twelve men. Jesus did not look for them at the best theological schools nor among the scholars but from Galilee. He chose common people - men who would not have preconceived religious ideas but would be open to His teaching.

THE TWELVE AS TEMPLES

Jesus worked for three and a half years at forming these twelve leaders. He taught these men to become temples of the living God. He gave practical teaching, *"Jesus answered and said to them, 'Destroy this temple, and in three days I will raise it up.' Then the Jews said, 'It has taken forty-six years to build this temple, and will You raise it up in three days?' But He was speaking of the temple of His body" (John 2:19-21).*

The Apostles knew what the Lord was talking about. Our lives are houses of God and we should take care of them to remain full of His presence. The Apostle Paul said: *"Or do you not know that your body is the temple of the Holy Spirit who is in you, whom you have from God, and you are not your own? For you were bought at a price; therefore glorify God in your body and in your spirit, which are God's" (1 Corinthians 6:19-20).*

MINISTERED TO IN ORDER TO MINISTER

The twelve should go through a process of inner healing and deliverance because those who have not received ministry are unable to minister to others. Through ministry we can confront sin until the person decides to overcome it. On many occasions, we have found that theological concepts are a blockage to the person receiving their full freedom in Christ. It is essential to keep in regular contact with those being discipled (the twelve), so that the ministry will be continuous. My suggestion is that you meet at least once a week, then you will be able to discern what kind of bondages people might have.

We have the example of the Apostle Peter who was commended by Jesus for his openness to receive a revelation directly from the Father (Matthew 16:17). Not long afterwards he called Jesus apart and began to advise him: *"Lord; this shall not happen to you" (Matthew 16:22)*. This was the work of Satan trying to oppose the Lord Jesus and His work at the cross of Calvary. Jesus rebuked Peter saying: *"Get behind Me, Satan! You are an offence to Me, for you are not mindful of the things of God, but the things of men" (Matthew 16:23)*. Then He used this opportunity to leave four clear principles in the lives of the Apostles *(Matthew 16:24-26):*

- *Whoever wants to be My disciple cannot be concerned about himself.*
- *Whoever wants to be My disciple should take his cross and follow Me.*
- *Whoever loses his life because of Me shall actually save it. Though many think that to serve the Lord is a waste of their life they are so far from the truth. The abundant life can only be enjoyed when Jesus rules us.*
- *Do not be selfish. The person who is concerned with their own external well-being will not be able to pay the price to rescue their soul.*

Jesus made the most of the time He had with the Twelve to shape their characters. Only after His death and resurrection did Jesus entrust them with what we now know as *The Great Commission.* He told them: *"Go therefore and make disciples of all the nations, baptising them in the name of the Father and of the Son and of the Holy Spirit, teaching them to observe all things that I have commanded you; and lo, I am with you always, even to the end of the age" (Matthew 28:19-20).*

The Lord Jesus, when He was on earth, won the greatest battle of all. The salvation of mankind depended on this victory. Even though He was divine and eternal, Jesus did not face the enemy as God but as Man. In this human form He overcame temptation and the fear of death. In the power of the Holy Spirit, Jesus faced death and rose again triumphant and victorious. Then, after His resurrection, He appeared to His twelve Apostles and told them: *"All authority has been given to Me in heaven and on earth" (Matthew 28:18).* Jesus fulfilled all that the Father had set out for Him. His will was that none would be lost but that all should repent of their sins. Jesus was even prepared to lay down His own life for this. He said, *"Greater love has no one than this, than to lay down his life for his friends" (John 16:13)* Jesus demonstrated how much He loved each one of His sheep by giving His own life for them. The Lord knew that His mission was not complete if the army He formed was not to continue His mission. That is why He told His disciples to go and make disciples of all nations. As the Father sent Jesus into the world - giving Him a specific mission that Jesus fulfilled with so much love - so He wants each one of us to fulfil the mission that is given to us. Then all of mankind will be redeemed. Each believer should commit to seeing this happen. God gave us the responsibility to reproduce life. Jesus Christ said: *"It is the Spirit who gives life; the flesh profits nothing. The words I speak to you are spirit, and they are life" (John 6:63).*

WINNING SOULS

Though the angels would like to preach the gospel, the Lord has reserved this privilege for His servants. The angel that appeared to Cornelius told him: *"Now send men to Joppa, and send back Simon whose surname is Peter" (Acts 10:5).*

Believers have the words of life on their lips! The Lord said through Ezekiel, *"Behold, all souls are Mine; The soul of the father as well as the soul of the son is Mine; The soul who sins shall die" (Ezekiel 18:4).* And Paul said: *"...for all have sinned and fall short of the glory of God" (Romans 3:23).*

Paul was conscious that the only way that humanity could be redeemed was for believers to share their faith. This is our responsibility as Christians and we should take it seriously. Paul also said: *"I am a debtor both to Greeks and to barbarians, both to wise and to unwise. So, as much as is in me, I am ready to preach the gospel to you who are in Rome also" (Romans 1:14-15).* When Paul says: *"as for me, I am ready"*, he is saying that we should imitate his example. Everyone who has got to know Jesus Christ as the Lord and Saviour has also acquired a debt towards the world. The commitment is that, as I was reached by the gospel of Jesus Christ, in the same way I should make every effort to reach others with the gospel. For our work to be effective we should be well prepared and we should be like soldiers, handling the word of truth diligently and with precision.

Experience has taught us that those who go through the discipleship process in a proper way find it easy to be soul winners. The twelve have to know about evangelistic work. They should have strategies to reach non-believers because their goal is to attract and then consolidate them. Men should know how to reach businessmen through leadership seminars and make sure that the atmosphere in the cell is such that the new men won't feel strange but comfortable. The youth should have strategies that will reach the youth. The music, dance and the atmosphere of the venue are important. The teaching should be specific for the youth, remembering that some of them are studying in college or university.

The women are also committed to sharing with other women, and I know that God is honouring the ministry of the women now. That is why there is a special anointing for them to develop their ministry in an extraordinary way. I am certain that God will continue to give us strategies until the whole world is filled with the glory of the Lord. The couples also feel very comfortable when they find a group of people that they can share their joys and sorrows with. It brings great satisfaction when these couples become God's instruments for the restoration of families. But even more so when they consolidate a new believer and reproduce in them the vision that the Lord entrusted to them. The twelve should develop their work homogeneously: a youth should win a youth, a man should win another man, a woman win another woman, couples win other couples and the children win other children. When we work homogeneously the reproduction is greater and takes place more quickly. In this way we can win people from all over the city and not be limited to just one specific area.

the ladder of success
a practical guide

THE CELL STRATEGY

The church should concentrate on cells, leaders being prepared for the work. In cell church each person, man or woman, youth or adult, professional or worker, has the opportunity to reach all their spiritual potential.

EFFECTIVE PASTORING

Many are involved, and it is more effective than when pastoring is left to one person.

CHURCH GROWTH

There should be growth when the transition is taking place. In other words, when a 'traditional' church moves towards becoming a cell church the back door is closed and people stop leaving the church that way. The church becomes a church without walls and the work of God is not limited. Every person has the opportunity to put into practice in their cell what they have learned. It is easy to see the abilities of each one of the cell members.

Relationships are strengthened. The secret for success is that people learn to relate to each other.

Commitment increases. The cell increases opportunities for participation in the ministry by all believers. They will become equipped to develop the vision that the Lord has entrusted to them.

The church remains alive. A cell church endures because it does not depend on a venue or building but it has no boundaries.

DEFINITIONS OF CELLS

From the various points of view:

Business
It is the basic unit of a structure. Each unit (or group) functions separately within the organisation.

Ideological
It is a small, organised group of people.

Chemical
It is a vessel in which chemical reactions take place. Its energy is transformed into electricity.

Biological
It is a fundamental unit of all living creatures. The cell is the smallest living unit. It has the capacity to multiply itself. It feeds itself, grows and reproduces, with each new cell having the same functions and characteristics as the original. Cells have different forms and sizes according to their purpose. There are cells which die immediately when their nucleus is attacked (as with the AIDS virus), and others which die when the attack begins in any other part of the cell (as in cancer).

THE BIOLOGICAL AND SPIRITUAL CELL

Biological Cell	Spiritual Cell
Internal changes	
Centromere	Leader
Nucleus	Host's home
Chromosome	Participation in the cell
Chromosome divides itself	The leader gets his disciples
Increase of chromosome	The group grows
Chromosome looks for a position	The leader and disciple work together
The nucleus breaks	Members ready to open new cells
Centromere and chromosome are defined	Positions are defined with one goal
External Changes	
The cell loses its external appearance	There should be a manifestation of the fruit of multiplication, with the commitment of another host
Semistrangulation of the cell	The new host opens his house to start a new cell
New nucleus are formed with its own centromere	New meetings begin with new people and new leader

WHY HAVE THE CELLS BEEN SUCCESSFUL?

Is it because of dynamic leadership?
Is it because of its impressive music and worship?
Is it because of excellent reading material?
Is it because of signs and wonders?
Is it because of the stimulating Bible study?
Is it because of its close fellowship?
Is it because of deep and transparent relationships?

All of these factors can contribute to the success of the cell but, without doubt, the most important element is the presence of the Holy Spirit at each meeting. How is a basic Christian community successful? Christ's presence is the DNA of the cell. In a biological cell DNA (Deoxyribonucleic acid) is the original action plan, the single most important force, the genetic code, the information and the catalyst that tells the cell how to grow and develop.

Jesus promised that He would be with His followers in His Church and that He would clothe it with power. The whole nature of the cell changes when He is the only focus. He, as the Head, starts to guide the cell. He grants its members spiritual gifts and fills them with His power. It is His presence that liberates the leadership, the music, gifts, the reading material, the Bible study, the communion and relationships. Jesus Himself is the essential factor in the life of His community on earth.

Spiritual Concept: God always works with individuals or complete family groups. After creating the first couple He ordered, *"Go forth and multiply."* This was the method established by the Creator to propagate the human race on earth.

WHY GOD DECIDED TO USE THE CELL

Herbert Butterfield said, *"The strongest organic unit in the history of the world appears to be the one we call the cell because it multiplies itself, without any faults. It is exceptionally difficult to destroy. It preserves its intensity of local life while larger organisations quickly disappear when they are weakened at their nucleus, It can challenge the power of governments, It is the effective tool to demolish every 'status quo'. It does not matter if we choose early Christianity, Calvinism in the 16th Century, or modern Communism, this seems to be the best way in which a group of people can open a new chapter in the history of civilisation."*

PURPOSES OF THE CELLS

Jesus told them, *"For where two or three come together in my name, I am there in their midst"* (Matthew 18:20).

The Church is the body of Christ. The body is made up of cells. Christ is the DNA of the cell. What makes the cell important is the presence of the living Christ in it. Therefore each cell is a vital part of the body of Christ and together they make up the foundations of the Church itself. Although the Church unites for big celebrations, it is in the cells that the Church is made known. The purity of its life, the strength of its transforming power, its power to penetrate society, its influence to change values, its evangelistic vigour, its service of the community and its determination to plant the kingdom of God on earth are all manifest through the cell.

Let us see, then, some of the purposes of the cell:

- *Experience the life and presence of Christ*
- *Offer care to the new believer and help him in the first steps of his Christian life*
- *Provide fellowship and pastoring to the members of the cell*
- *Penetrate the community with the message of salvation. The cell is the main arm of evangelism in the Church*
- *Provide social assistance to the needy*

the ladder of success
a practical guide

- *Offer opportunity for the formation of leadership through experience*
- *Serve the community with acts of love in needy areas*

SPECIFIC PURPOSES

WIN. Evangelising those that are outside the group. The cell must reach the lost. Its goal is to carry out the Great Commission, which is the desire of God's heart.

CONSOLIDATE. Strengthen the faith of the new believers helping them with their first steps in the Christian life.

DISCIPLE. The whole process of training is continued until the people enter the School of Leaders so that in a year they will become cell leaders.

SEND. If the work is done correctly through the cells, there will be more effective growth because of the anointing for multiplication.

DYNAMICS OF THE CELL

Every cell must pass through a process which goes from its creation to multiplication into twelve more. Ensure that in your cell there is not duplication but multiplication.

MEETING-PLACE

Houses, offices, schools and any place where it is possible to meet with a small group every week. Day and Time: Make sure it is convenient for both the leader of the cell and the host.

Duration: We suggest maximum of one hour
What should we do in the cell meeting?

1. Welcome
2. Initial prayer
3. Testimonies
4. Teaching of the Word
5. Prayer for the different needs
6. Offering
7. Final prayer

Welcome

Reception. As the people arrive for the cell meeting the leader, host and the rest of the group should greet them warmly showing love and interest.

Presentation

New cell members should be introduced to everyone making them fill as part of the family.

Start

The leader should open the cell with an 'ice breaker', encouraging everyone to participate. It is important to create a family atmosphere within the cell. This will strengthen friendship relationships.

Teaching

This is a key moment when God will speak through His written Word, the Holy Bible. Jesus said, *"The words that I speak to you are spirit, and they are life" (John 6:63).*

PURPOSES:

1. **Convert.** *Take the non-believer to the point of experiencing conversion by showing the truths of the Gospel of Jesus Christ.*

2. **Edify.** *Introduce the new believer to the Word, helping him to understand the principles of the kingdom of God into which he has now entered.*

3. **Form Character.** *Shape the character of the cell members so that they become like Jesus (2 Corinthians 3:18).*

4. **Form Values.** *Form Christian values in the lives of the cell members, building them up through the Word of God.*

The message preached by the pastor the previous Sunday could be used. Also, a Rhema word from a leader of each net (men, women, youth) can be addressed in the cell.

EXPOSITION. Review the principal points from the message. Study the Bible and apply it to their lives. Lead the cell members to arrive at their own conclusions.

Examine actual behaviour in the light of biblical truths. Lead the cell members to make a decision to adjust their lifestyles in accordance with the word they have studied. Give opportunities for reflection and response so that everyone becomes not only a hearer but also a doer of the Word. Encourage the cell to develop a life of prayer in which God can unfold His Word to them.

OFFERING. The offering is the opportunity given by God for all the cell members to express their commitment through their giving. It is important to teach the law of sowing and reaping, good stewardship and the blessings for those who are faithful with their offerings and tell about the curses for those who are stingy with God.

PRAYER. Pray for the person who should occupy the empty chair and who is still absent.

Intercession is presenting ourselves on behalf of the needs of others. It is to pray for the needs of the cell members and to cry out for the fulfilment of the goals. It is a covering prayer for the pastors and leaders of the church, placing a hedge of protection around the church and our cell. It is to pray for those in leadership that the Lord would give them boldness in the preaching of the Word. It is to pray for those in authority that are leading the nation. It is to commit ourselves to pray that Israel would be restored to peace and to cry out for Christ's return.

SUGGESTIONS FOR AN EFFECTIVE CELL

- *Be punctual.*
- *Be well dressed, clean and with good breath.*
- *Be polite and gracious. Do not be impolite or forceful.*
- *Encourage everyone to participate.*
- *Always show gratitude to the host.*
- *Speak loud enough so that all can hear.*
- *Fully prepare for everything you want to share. Remember that what you want to happen in the cell has to be conquered first in the secret place.*
- *Always motivate the cell to bring new friends to the following meeting.*
- *Do not be afraid to pray for miracles to happen.*
- *Ensure you maintain a good testimony.*
- *Never borrow money from any member of the cell.*
- *Be respectful and courteous to every member of the cell.*
- *Avoid familiarity that could be misunderstood.*
- *When bringing a person of the opposite sex, ask somebody to go with you.*
- *When you have to visit a member of the cell take someone with you. All visits should start and finish on time.*
- *Do not delegate responsibilities to people who are not ready for them.*
- *Never discuss anything that a cell member has told you in confidence.*
- *Do not listen to negative comments about other people.*
- *Be an example of faith to all the members of the cell. Without faith it is impossible to please God.*

Even though you may have a model cell that has already been proven by its results, if the element of faith is missing the hands of God will be tied and you will not be able to see the results that you yearn for in your ministry. But if you put your heart into it and faithfully follow each of the steps that we have presented in this manual I can promise that your ministry will take on another dimension: that of conquering your city and nation for Christ.

BIBLIOGRAPHY

Dream and You will win the World - Experiences
Encounter Series -
Bible Studies for the School of Leaders
Successful Leadership through the Twelve -
Aspects of the Vision
As Firm as the Rock Series -
Fundamental Doctrine according to Hebrews 6
> Book 1 - *Knowing the Truth*
> Book 2 - *Repentance, the Starting*
> *Point for Blessing*
> Book 3 - *Entering the Faith Realm*
> Book 4 - *Immersed in His Spirit*
> Book 5 - *His Hand is upon Me*
> Book 6 - *Revived by His Power*
> Book 7 - *Before His Throne*
Cesar Castellanos

**Consolidation, An Effective Process for Making
Disciples -** Consolidation Manual
Strengthening My Steps - Post-Encounter Material
Claudia Fajardo

For the School of Leaders
1. Summary of Doctrine for Levels 1,2, and 3
2. Summary of Lectures for Levels 2 and 3
3. Summary for the Youth, Men's and Women's
Nets - First Level.

Card for the School of Leaders
(First and Second Levels - for the disciple).

Vilit Editorial
January 2001 - Bogota - Colombia
Edivilit@impsat.net.co

the ladder of success
a practical guide